Depreciation Reports in British Columbia

Depreciation Reports in British Columbia

The Strata Lots Owners Guide to Selecting Your Provider and Understanding Your Report

Jeremy Bramwell, AACI, P.App, RI

Keith Davis

Strata Reserve Planning

CONTENTS

Introduction

Chapter 1 - The Basics of Reserve Planning — 4

Chapter 2 - Why Do We Do Depreciation Reports? — 8

Chapter 3 – Who Are the Players? — 11

Chapter 4 – Determining Your Needs — 25

Chapter 5 – Reports Commonly Confused with Depreciation Reports — 39

Chapter 6 – Property Managers and Suppliers — 44

Chapter 7 – Conflicts of Interest — 46

Chapter 8 – The Fee Is Not Everything — 49

Chapter 9 – When to Order the Report — 51

Chapter 10 – Proposal Review Analysis — 54

Chapter 11 – The Component Inventory — 60

Chapter 12 – Collecting Documents — 64

Chapter 13 – Classes of Depreciation Reports — 78

Chapter 14 – Selection of the Components — 84

Chapter 15 - Separation of the Components — 93

Chapter 16 – What to Expect at the Inspection — 95

CONTENTS

- Chapter 17 - Funding Principles 100
- Chapter 18 – Funding Choices 102
- Chapter 19 – The Financial Variables 104
- Chapter 20 – The Benchmark Analysis 114
- Chapter 21 – Measuring the Financial Health of My Complex 119
- Chapter 22 – Generally Accepted Funding Plan Models 124
- Chapter 23 – Making a Recommended Funding Plan 131

APPENDIX A - TERMS AND DEFINITIONS 137

Copyright © 2024 by Jeremy Bramwell

All rights reserved. No part of this book may be reproduced in any manner whatsoever without written permission except in the case of brief quotations embodied in critical articles and reviews.

First Printing, May 1, 2023
ISBN: 978-1-7388490-0-0 (No longer available)

Second Printing May 1, 2024
Updated to meet all legislated changes as of May 1, 2024
ISBN: 978-1-7388490-2-4

ACKNOWLEDGEMENT

I would like to thank the Real Estate of Canada for teaching me how to write a Depreciation Report. This training, combined with the standards of the Appraisal Institute of Canada and USA-based reserve planning organizations, led to an understanding of a Standards-based methodology used in my business and this book.

I would be remiss if I did not thank my past and current staff, who have worked to improve our approach, but especially my Technical Director and friend, Keith Davis, for his assistance in the book.

Lastly, I must thank my wife, Giselle and my son, Ross, for their endless support in writing this book.

Introduction

I have been in the trenches of preparing Depreciation Reports for British Columbian strata lot owners, councils, and property managers.

Since 2011, as one of BC's first Certified Reserve Planners (CRP), I have been completing Depreciation Reports. In 2015, I contributed to the RRFP (Registered Reserve Fund Planner Program) course materials at the University of British Columbia (UBC). This highly esteemed educational program is now being used for all CRPs across Canada. More recently, in 2021-22, I was asked to be the Subject Matter Expert for Functional Depreciation Reports for a BC Housing Policy Branch subcommittee.

When I started my reserve planning firm, Strata Reserve Planning, I decided that a Standards-based approach was the best way to serve our clients. In 2012, I wrote CARSS (Commonly Accepted Reserve Study Standards), an internal document of generally accepted standards for use in our reports. This document was updated in 2014 when the Appraisal Institute of Canada brought out the only specific reserve planning standards in Canada. In 2017, we designed our proprietary Depreciation Report software using this approach. Our experience and these standards are the basis for this book.

The Current Situation

Put simply, the British Columbia reserve planning industry is a mess. Most Owners, Strata Councils, and Property Managers do not seem to understand the types of reports or the strength of each type of provider. Standards are minimal, and terminology is used interchangeably. Financial modelling is not based on realistic scenarios, leading to unexpected financial hardships. Benchmarking the financial health of complexes is not understood or completed in many cases. In summary, Strata Corporations in BC are poorly served.

The same problems occurred decades before reserve planners established professional organizations in the USA. These groups created standards for content and disclosure, shared terminology, and standardized financial modelling. Reserve Adequacy (or Percent Funded) became the accepted method to measure the financial health of strata/condominium developments.

This situation in BC will continue until Canadian professional providers form their own organizations with standards. Until those changes occur, a book like this is a necessary tool.

Who is This Book For?

This book is for Strata Councils and Owners looking to obtain a Depreciation Report or wanting to understand them.

Section One is about making the best choices before signing a Contract. It covers what council members should know before ordering and reviewing a proposal. For many readers, this is the most crucial part of the book as it allows decision-makers to understand the legislation, the types of providers, their strengths and weaknesses, the role of specialists, when to order, and things to think about when reviewing proposals.

Section Two covers the physical inspection involved in a Depreciation Report. This information includes the required data and how components are selected and later separated into smaller groups.

Section Three covers financial assumptions and accepted reporting methodology. This includes a discussion that covers the common errors that impact the report's reliability.

Depreciation Reports in British Columbia is to assist Strata Councils and Owners in receiving an accurate and reliable Depreciation Report by making an informed choice about the provider, understanding how the planner prepared the report, and how to analyze the conclusions.

Section One

Choosing the Provider

Chapter 1 - The Basics of Reserve Planning

Reserve planning is the process of creating a Depreciation Report for Strata Corporations. But before the planning starts, we need to understand the meaning of the words used in this book. While some terminology is based on legislation, others are words used industry-wide, and some of the language used in this book is from my company. The appendix has a list of commonly used terms.

The first decision of any Strata Council is who will prepare the Depreciation Report. The purpose of Section One of this book is to assist in this decision, in choosing the best provider for your Strata Corporation.

"Qualified Persons" are people designated in the *Strata Property Act* as qualified to complete Depreciation Reports. These people and the firms that provide Depreciation Report services are called Planners or Providers.

Prior to April 22, 2024, the Strata Property Regulations 6.2 (6) stated that a "Qualified Person" meant:

"any person who has the knowledge and expertise to understand the individual components, scope and complexity of the Strata Corporation's common property, common assets and those parts of a strata lot or limited common property, or both, that the Strata Corporation is responsible to maintain or repair under the Act, the Strata Corporation's bylaws or an agreement with an owner and to prepare a depreciation report that complies with subsections (1) to (4)."

This regulation had been interpreted as meaning anyone, including members of the Strata Corporation, could complete the Depreciation Reports. Some did. This regulation led many unqualified people, from landscapers to road builders, to enter the business.

As of July 1, 2024, the Strata Property Regulations defines a "Qualified Person" as:

a. A professional engineer registered as a member in good standing with the Association of Professional Engineers and Geoscientists of the Province of British Columbia;

b. A person registered as an architect with the Architectural Institute of British Columbia;

c. A person designated Accredited Appraiser Canadian Institute (AACI) by the Appraisal Institute of Canada;

d. A Certified Reserve Planner (CRP) accredited by the Real Estate Institute of Canada;

   e. A person designated as a Professional Quantity Surveyor by the Canadian Institute of Quantity Surveyors and

   f. A person registered as an applied science technologist under the Professional Governance Act;

This change will restrict the number of people who can complete the Depreciation Report to those who should be more qualified. Chapters 3 and 4 discuss these six designations in more detail.

The *Strata Property Act* requires a Strata Corporation to have two bank accounts. The operating account is used for running the complex regularly, while the long-term reserve account, called the contingency reserve fund (CRF), is used to save money for significant future capital repairs, replacements, or renewals of components and assets.

A Depreciation Report identifies the condition of the common area components and assets, the replacement or renewal costs, and three Funding Plans to offset these future expenditures.

Components refer to items attached to the building, such as siding, roofing, doors, hallway carpeting, and landscaping.

Assets are a type of component not attached to the building that can be picked up and moved. They are commonly called Furniture, Fixtures, and Equipment (FF&E). This list includes items in the lobby, laundry room, gym, pool, kitchen, common areas, and guest suites. These will be covered more as we delve into more detail in Section 2.

A Funding Plan is the funding choices made to fund future expenditures. These choices include annual CRF contributions, interest earned, special levies, or loans. BC legislation mandates three funding plans, but usually, only one is recommended in a report. Chapters 17 and 18 discuss the types of funding plans.

Contributions are the monthly or annual fees collected by the Strata Corporation as part of the yearly budget for the CRF account. They exclude interest income, special levies, proceeds from a strata loan (borrowings), or transfers at the year-end from an operating budget surplus.

Income includes annual contributions, interest income, special levies, proceeds from a strata loan (borrowings), or transfers from the operating budget surplus at the year-end.

A Depreciation Report consists of two interrelated parts: the Physical and the Financial Analysis.

The Physical Analysis involves collecting documents and inspecting the building components and assets to determine the component inventory, physical condition analysis, and life estimates of the building components and assets, which the Strata Corporation must maintain. This is covered in Section Two.

The documents collected are based on the class of the Depreciation Report and the characteristics of the property. The initial report is the Comprehensive Depreciation Report, followed by the Updated Depreciation Report after the mandated five-year renewal period.

This information, when combined with a site inspection, results in the component inventory. The Component Inventory lists all the items in a Depreciation Report that the Strata Corporation is responsible for maintaining.

The Financial Analysis evaluates the Strata Corporation's CRF opening balance, history of contributions, prior interest income, and the projected expenses in the Benchmark Analysis to determine the recommended funding plan. This is covered in Section Three.

The Benchmark Analysis summarizes the component inventory, with the current and future replacement costs adjusted by the Construction Inflation Rate (CIR) and Investment Interest Rate (IIR). It also calculates the projected annual contribution if the owners have fully funded the Strata Corporation. This schedule is the key to assessing the financial state of the Strata Corporation and creating a recommended funding plan.

The IIR, the average interest rate of return from the CRF account, and the CIR are supplied from historical data. The replacement costs are derived from the market.

The recommended funding plan should increase the Strata Corporation's reserve fund status over the 30-year projection time frame, as measured by Reserve Adequacy (Percent Funded). Reserve Adequacy is the internationally accepted method of determining the financial strength of a Strata Corporation.

One of the largest misconceptions owners have is that the Depreciation Report's function is to estimate annual CRF contributions, so there are no special levies or special assessments.

A funding plan with no special levies would mean that the development is fully funded, meaning that the contributions are enough to pay for any renovations, replacements, or renewals in the 30-year projection period of the report. To be fully funded, the funding plan would also have sufficient money in the CRF, combined with a reasonable income level, to pay for expenses in the future beyond the 30-year projections.

No development in BC is fully funded, as the economic stress on the Strata Corporation owners would be too high.

So, what is the provider's goal if no Strata is fully funded?

Depreciation Report providers work to create a funding plan with a level of contributions and other income that would be acceptable to most Owners while meeting the Strata Corporation's requirements to maintain the development. As discussed in this book, this can be a tricky balance.

Chapter 2 - Why Do We Do Depreciation Reports?

British Columbia legislation requires Depreciation Reports because strata lot owners have done a less than adequate job saving for the future when allowed to do it themselves. But to be fair, there was no requirement to have a plan.

Between 1998 and 2009, the British Columbia government lent $671 million of interest-free loans for leaky condominiums. Some of this money is still outstanding. The reconstruction loan program was costly. If the BC government had to replicate that program today, the costs would be $3 to $5 billion. Having owners plan and save for their financial future makes more sense.

But it's not only Canadians who do not save.

Champlain Towers South
National Institute of Standards and Technology (US)

On June 24, 2021, Champlain Towers South, a 12-story condominium complex in the Miami suburb of Surfside, Florida, collapsed, causing the death of 98 people.

Later, it emerged that the CRF fees had stayed the same for ten years, and the owners had voted down special assessments to pay for the work shortly before the collapse. The building failed financially before it failed physically.

In 2009, the BC government made Depreciation Reports mandatory. However, the legislation had a clause allowing them to be deferred indefinitely. The government hoped that if the owners had a Depreciation Report, they would make reasonable decisions about saving for their financial future. In a conversation with one of the people who wrote this clause, the legislators thought that market forces would drive people to get reports. The opposite occurred: owners voted to defer them to save money. In 2024, it was estimated that less than 20% of the Strata Corporations in BC were compliant, meaning more than 80% had not had a Depreciation Report completed in the past three years.

On April 22, 2024, the BC Government removed the option to defer. All Strata corporations in BC must now get Depreciation Reports. The government has gone from hoping Strata Corporations would get one to ensuring they do.

If the Strata completed its last report on or after January 1, 2021, the next one is due five years after the previous report.

If the Strata never completed one, or the last report had an effective date before January 1, 2021, the location determines the deadline. For developments in the Capital Regional District (except the Gulf Islands) or the Lower Mainland, the Depreciation Report must be completed by July 1, 2026. For those on the Gulf Islands or anywhere else in British Columbia, the deadline is a year later, July 1, 2027.

A new Strata Corporation established after July 1, 2024, must obtain its first Depreciation Report within 2 years of the Strata's first AGM without any funding requirement from the developer. As of July 1, 2027, the Strata must obtain its first Depreciation Report within 18 months of its first AGM. However, the developer of these new complexes must have paid enough into the CRF to pay for the first Depreciation Report.

Like all provinces, British Columbia has regulations requiring legal or statutory requirements for the CRF account. Before November 1, 2023, the minimum balance in the CRF was 25% of the operating account. However, if the balance dropped below 25% of the annual budget, the Strata had to top it up by a maximum amount of 10% of the current operating budget.

In response, in January 2023, BC changed the statutory minimum annual contribution. As of November 1, 2023, the CRF annual contribution must be 10% of the annual operating budget. The ability to cap contributions at 25% of the operating fund was removed. This change may result in higher contributions from owners over time.

The problem with the statutory minimum is that inflation in the construction sector ranges between 5% and 15% annually. This is well above the 2% to 3% that Strata Corporations usually try to keep their budgets within; thus, any relationships between the operating and replacement costs have been lost.

In my experience, as the statutory minimum is tied to operating costs, any Strata Corporation that funds its CRF using this method will always contribute far less than necessary for proper building maintenance.

The government has not mandated that the Strata follow the recommended plan in the report. They still hope owners will use the Depreciation Report to make reasonable decisions about saving for their financial future.

There are developments where the Owners do not follow the recommended funding plan. Sometimes, the provider is at fault as the recommendations are unreasonable or there needs to be corrected data. Sometimes, the owners just do not like the conclusions. But, sometimes, the report was inappropriate as they hired the wrong type of provider.

The new legislation may help address the issue as part of the changes focuses on "Qualified Persons," that is, the providers who should be doing the reports. As discussed in the last chapter, the legislation had let anyone complete Depreciation Reports, but now the list is much more limited. The legislation and the list of qualified providers are now more closely aligned with nearly all provinces and states throughout North America.

Expertise is usually implied if a person has a designation and the designation is on the government-qualified list. And if they have a designation, most people assume that the provider will use a standards-based approach. However, the legislation does not focus on expertise or whether the provider follows commonly accepted Depreciation Report standards.

Part of the solution is making sure you get the right provider. It is up to the Strata Council to ensure that the provider has the expertise and follows reserve planning standards. The following chapters of the book aim to help readers make the best decision about the provider and the report type for their property.

Chapter 3 – Who Are the Players?

This chapter reviews the "who's who" in the industry, followed by the strengths and weaknesses of each type of the leading provider groups. This book will focus on those who have been designated as "Qualified Persons" in British Columbia. Following the narrative of this chapter, we have a more in-depth discussion of engineers, other types of providers, and specialized consultants. The information you will find in those chapters should lead you to a decision on the kind of provider that best fits your development needs.

Many people misunderstand providers' professional responsibility structure and who will work on their reports. In most situations, especially in a larger complex, not all the participants will be described in the legislation or the proposal. Without this knowledge, choosing a provider to meet the complex's needs is extremely hard. Council members need to investigate who will actually be doing the work.

Professionals generally fall into the following groups:

"Qualified Persons," commonly called Designated Persons, are those the provincial legislation has deemed qualified to complete a Depreciation Report. They must sign the report and take responsibility for its contents. For example, an AACI (Accredited Appraiser Canadian Institute) is a member of the Appraisal Institute of Canada and is qualified in the legislation in BC and generally across Canada.

Unapproved designated people are those with a designation not listed in the provincial legislation for Depreciation Reports but belong to the same professional organization as a designated person. For example, a CRA (Certified Residential Appraiser) is a member of the Appraisal Institute of Canada and is an unapproved designated person.

A Candidate is someone in training to become a designated person. They can work on a file and sign it under the supervision of a designated person.

Co-signing is when the senior designated person in a report agrees with the conclusion of the work completed by the unapproved designated person or the candidate. Both parties sign the report, taking equal responsibility.

Inspectors are not in the same professional organization as the designated person. Still, due to a specific skill set or remote location, they are allowed by the organization to complete an inspection that their member signs. The inspector must have insurance to work with any professional organization. Also, the inspector must be named for the work they completed but will not co-sign the report. In general, inspectors are limited to the physical inspection portion of the report.

Specialists have unique skill sets, like roof inspectors or thermographic imaging consultants. Within the Depreciation Report environment, they are sometimes required to provide an independent report in their area of expertise. The report conclusions are added to the Depreciation Report as part of the physical and financial analysis.

These services are usually optional in a report. If the proposal recommends these services, the Strata Council should seriously consider the reasoning. Sometimes, the strata complex insurance company may want information from a specialist. In other cases, the Strata Council may request input from a specialist, like a mechanical engineer, in the case of a geothermal heating system.

Clerical assistance is a term for the support staff. Their work differs from the groups named above as they are limited to information that does not need analysis, like the client's name, the property address, etc. They are not named in the report nor sign it.

So why should council members care about who works on the Depreciation Report?

If you are paying a premium price, you should expect the participation of qualified people.

Many problems have arisen when the designated people are highlighted in the proposal as a selling point. Then, the owners are surprised when, in their opinion, unknown and barely qualified candidates show up to do the inspection. I have had clients tell me that it felt like the last provider was using their complex as a training site.

When engaging a Depreciation Report provider, the Strata Council should understand who will complete the inspection and their background. If the inspector is a candidate, it is reasonable to insist that the supervisory designated person accompany them for the entire inspection.

Another vital issue to review is the professional standards they must follow. Most designated groups have a code of conduct or ethical standards. I am referring to professional standards used specifically for completing Depreciation Reports.

The US-based designations discussed later in the chapter, the Reserve Specialist (RS) follows the National Reserve Study Standards (NRSS), and the Professional Reserve Analyst (PRA) follows the APRA Standards of Practice. These standards are the most comprehensive in North America.

The only specific Depreciation Report Standards in Canada are from the Appraisal Institute of Canada, meaning all AACI-designated providers must follow them.

As of the writing of this book, the Real Estate Institute of Canada teaches the accepted methodology for completing reports but has no specific Depreciation Report standards. I understand there has been a push to introduce standards, but this effort has failed over the past several years.

This lack of organization-driven reserve planning standards does not mean that professionals in groups without specific standards do not follow them. It's well known that some providers follow other organizations' methodologies and standards.

Strata Councils need to ask for a copy of the providers' standards.

The following pages cover the key information of each of the main groups of providers that should be considered when selecting providers. The default motto for many looking to order a Depreciation Report is *"Let's get an Engineer...."* So, we will cover them first.

Registered Engineer, Designation: P.Eng.

Description:

There are six groups of engineers, but not all engineers are the same or qualified to do a Depreciation Report.

The most common engineers within reserve planning are civil and structural engineers. Other types used in Depreciation Reports are mechanical engineers, electrical engineers, and, in some cases, chemical engineers. A list of each engineering specialty follows:

Candidates:

Candidates or undesignated engineers must identify themselves as EITs (Engineers in Training).

Reserve Planning Standards:

No.

Inspection Specialists:

There is a full range of specialists, such as BES (Building Envelope Specialists), Applied Science Technologist (AScT), Certified Technician (CTech), Registered Roof Observers (RRO), and elevator consultants, who work with engineers and others.

Co-signing:

Engineering firms that conduct reserve planning usually operate with an engineer overseeing the operation and EIT (Engineers in Training) or other inspection specialists doing the actual analysis. Candidates' work must be co-signed by a supervising designated engineer (P.Eng.).

Liability Insurance:

Engineers are self-regulated and must have liability insurance for the work they complete.

A more detailed review of engineers expected to work on a Depreciation Report is on the following pages.

Engineering Specialities

Civil:

Civil engineering is considered the oldest engineering discipline and focuses on the design of the complex. You would choose a civil engineer for designs and plans for site grading, retaining walls, drainage and sewer, stormwater, and septic tanks. Civil engineers usually handle cost estimates, calculations, documentation, building code reviews, and construction administration.

Structural:

Structural engineering is a specialty within civil engineering. Structural engineers are required for new condominium developments, structural evaluations, warranty reviews, remodelling or additions to existing structures, and issues relating to decks and patios. A structural engineer is also required for rebuilding after a fire, foundations and underground parking, structural calculations, calculations for supports or attachments for safety or roof equipment, HVAC, or solar panels.

Within reserve planning, structural engineers would be engaged in a situation where there is a concern about foundation integrity, concrete buildings with a visible indicator of construction flaws or the owners wanting an exterior review. Once an issue is identified, the council would add civil engineers to the team.

The general rule is that the more complex a building envelope is, the more likely a structural engineer is required for a Depreciation Report to help identify potential structural problems.

When the envelope is minimal in complexity, or the building is wood-framed, a civil or structural engineer is likely unnecessary, as other providers can supply reliable assessments at a lower cost.

Mechanical:

Mechanical engineers design and manufacture machines, equipment, final products, and parts that influence the design of other systems. In a condominium complex, mechanical engineers are required as project managers for sizeable renewal projects or to properly maintain complex air-conditioning systems, turbines, and pumps. Mechanical engineers should evaluate these types of components for Depreciation Reports.

Mechanical engineers are not required if there are no complex mechanical systems or when HVAC and elevator consultants are available for reliable specialized assessments. Even if an engineer is needed for the evaluation, they often work in a team approach with other types of providers.

Electrical:

Within a Depreciation Report context, electrical engineers oversee the testing of electrical equipment and control systems, including transmission, sub-transmission and distribution lines, substations, capacitors, relays, circuit breakers, transformers, lighting equipment, generators, and related items. They also assist in reviewing power loads, the required capacity of services and installations, and the impact of added load on the system. Finally, they can help mechanical engineers with the electrical implications of upgraded mechanical systems.

Typically, they would be engaged where there is a complex electrical system, specifically a high-rise development. An electrical engineer is optional if there are no complex electrical systems, or consultants can supply specialized services like thermographic imaging for the low-rise or townhome breaker boxes.

Chemical:

Chemical engineering, or process engineering, ensures that processes are designed with the utmost safety while considering social, environmental, and business needs. Chemical engineers have a minimal place in Depreciation Reports. They are typically brought on to assist when a complex has a treatment centre for its community water or community wastewater system.

As the previous descriptions show, engineers may be the default choice, but they are often not required.

The alternative options are provided on the following pages.

Registered Architect, Designation: Architect

Description:

Registered architects are educated in the design of buildings to meet the building codes, as well as design restorations and renovations.

Candidates:

Architects in training must identify themselves as Interim Architects.

Reserve Planning Standards:

No.

Inspection Specialists:

Not Applicable.

Co-signing:

A supervising Architect must co-sign interim architects' work.

Liability Insurance:

Architects are self-regulated and must have liability insurance for the work they complete.

Accredited Appraiser Canadian Institute, Designation: AACI

Description:

The Appraisal Institute of Canada (AIC) awards its most senior designation (AACI) across Canada. It is the preeminent appraisal group in Canada. They are highly educated in the design of buildings for valuation purposes.

Candidates:

Appraisers can use Candidates to assist them. Candidates are not commonly used for Depreciation Report assignments as they usually lack the required inspection experience.

Reserve Planning Standards:

The Appraisal Institute of Canada (AIC) is the only Canadian organization with specific reserve planning standards. In 2014, the AIC instituted these standards as part of its governing document, the Canadian Uniform Standards of Professional Appraisal Practice (CUSPAP).

Inspection Specialists:

The AIC has a policy allowing approved inspectors to complete physical inspections only under limited circumstances.

Co-signing:

While the AIC permits residential appraisers or CRAs (Certified Residential Appraisers) to complete Depreciation Reports, no provincial legislation qualifies them. Like candidates, CRAs would have to be co-signed by a senior appraiser.

Liability Insurance:

The AIC is self-insured, with a liability insurance program for members who complete work as outlined in CUSPAP.

Certified Reserve Planner, Designation: CRP

Description:

The Real Estate Institute of Canada (REIC) has an education program for the Certified Reserve Planner (CRP) designation. The program teaches the principles behind reserve planning and the methodology for completing a Depreciation Report.

In 2018, the REIC suspended the CRP program due to the sudden death of one of the two instructors and the retirement of the other. In late 2021, the REIC signed an agreement with the University of BC (UBC) to utilize the UBC distance education reserve planning program.

Candidates:

No.

Reserve Planning Standards:

None.

Inspection Specialists:

None

Co-signing:

No.

Liability Insurance:

Members must get private insurance. The REIC has a third-party liability insurance program for anyone with the CRP designation, but insurance is not required to maintain the designation.

Applied Science Technologist Designation: AScT

Description:

The Applied Science Technologist (AScT) designation is a provincial designation held by the Applied Science Technologists and Technicians of BC (ASTTBC). Until 2021, they were self-governing but are now governed by the Provincial Governance Act (PGA). Education is provided through various institutions across BC.

The designation allows for the specialties of architecture, civil, construction, electrical, electronics, instrumentation, mechanical, petroleum, and technology.

When looking at an AScT, please confirm that the designated person's specialty meets your development needs. Most developments should focus on those with Architectural, Civil, and Construction specialties.

The ASTTBC designations of Registered Reserve Fund Analyst (Limited) (RRFAL) and Registered Reserve Fund Analyst (RRFA) are not recognized under provincial legislation as being qualified. If the person also has an AScT designation, they may be qualified.

Candidates:

Applied Science Technologists can use Candidates to assist them.

Reserve Planning Standards:

None.

Inspection Specialists:

None.

Co-signing:

No.

Liability Insurance:

ASTTBC members are provided with liability insurance for the work they complete.

Quantity Surveyor, Designation: PQS

Description:

The Canadian Institute of Quantity Surveyors (CIQS) offers the Professional Quantity Surveyor (PQS) designation. The PQS manages the contractual and financial side and lifespan analysis in Canada. They inspect buildings under construction, but the inspection of existing structures is much more limited.

Candidates:

There is a candidate system for this designation, but it is rare for a quantity surveyor to complete a Depreciation Report like architects.

Reserve Planning Standards:

None.

Inspection Specialists:

None.

Co-signing:

The CIQS has a junior designation called Construction Estimator Certified (CEC), which is certified for cost estimation only. Therefore, candidates are only sometimes engaged in a Depreciation Report. A senior surveyor must co-sign candidates.

Liability Insurance:

Quantity Surveyors have a liability program for the services they provide.

Another well-known Canadian designation and two US designations need some discussion. However, British Columbia does not recognize them.

Reserve Fund Planning Program, Designation: RFPP

Description:

The Reserve Fund Planning Program (RFPP) is a national program designed by UBC. Like the CRP program, it focuses on teaching how to complete a Depreciation Report.

Candidates:

No.

Reserve Planning Standards:

As a designation certificate program, there are no governing association membership requirements. The lack of an association means there are no reserve planning standards.

Inspection Specialists:

None.

Co-signing:

No.

Liability Insurance:

Members must get private insurance. However, insurance is not required to maintain the designation.

The new CRP education program is the same training as the Reserve Fund Planning Program (RFPP). The RFPP designation is a national program designed by UBC. Like the CRP program, it focuses on teaching how to complete a Depreciation Report. The RFPP designation is recognized in other provinces, so its exclusion from the BC list of qualified people surprised many.

Reserve Specialist, Designation: RS

Description:

The Community Association Institute (CAI) RS designation is universally accepted in the US. The National Reserve Study Standards (NRSS) were instituted in 1996, with the latest revisions in 2016. The NRSS and the APRA Standards of Practice are the basis for the analysis discussed in this book.

There are no known RS designations in Canada, but their influence extends to Canada, as the 2014 AIC Standards for Reserve Planning appear to be very similar to the NRSS.

Candidates:

No.

Reserve Planning Standards:

The National Reserve Study Standards (NRSS) govern all members and defines some terms regarding Depreciation Reports.

Inspection Specialists:

None.

Co-signing:

No.

Liability Insurance:

Members must get private insurance, and insurance is required to maintain the designation.

Professional Reserve Analysts, Designation: PRA

Description:

The PRA designation is an alternative option in the US. The Association of Professional Reserve Analysts (APRA) standards in the US are generally the same as the NRSS and have been around since the 1990s.

Some PRAs exist in Canada, and this credential is a secondary designation for many of them. The APRA offers a series of ongoing industry courses that are not accessible by other organizations.

Candidates:

No.

Reserve Planning Standards:

The APRA Standards of Practice are the Standards for all Association of Professional Reserve Analysts members and define some terms regarding Depreciation Reports.

Inspection Specialists:

None.

Co-signing:

No.

Liability Insurance:

Members must get private insurance, and insurance is required to maintain the designation.

Now that we have covered the Provider options, the following chapters will assist the reader in determining the best choice based on their needs.

Chapter 4 – Determining Your Needs

To utilize these qualified people to their fullest extent, Strata Corporations must review their needs before looking at potential suppliers. This chapter will review the two main types of reports and what kind of provider is required based on who can meet the complex's needs.

These are the three questions a Strata Council usually asks when considering a Provider.

1. Do I need an engineer?
2. When can I use a non-engineer provider?
3. When do I need a Specialist?

The answer to the first question has two parts. The first part is whether the Strata Corporation needs invasive testing, known as an Engineered Depreciation Report. The second part is whether using an engineer is mandatory, meaning the choice is taken from the hands of the Strata Council by legislation.

Once the first question is answered, the answers to the second and third questions will be answered in this systematic approach to determining the best type of provider for your Depreciation Report.

The Two Types of Depreciation Reports

The first choice Strata Councils need to make is whether they want a **Functional** or **Engineered** Depreciation Report.

I have spent over a decade helping people understand the difference between the two types of Depreciation Reports. Decision makers need to understand the difference and what is being proposed.

Functional Depreciation Reports rely on the client's historical operational information, plans and financial data. After reviewing these data, the provider completes an inspection to determine the condition of the components and assets. Then, the report is completed.

The same methodology is undertaken in an **Engineered Depreciation Report**, except there will be invasive testing. As there is invasive testing, a registered engineer must sign the test results and the report.

Invasive testing is when the building envelope is punctured by drilling a test hole, cutting into the roof for a probe, or cutting a wall patch. Invasive testing can also involve disassembling machinery to look inside. If you want invasive testing, the report must be completed by an engineer or a firm with a specialized consultant.

Functional-type reports do not include invasive testing.

The truth is, due to the liability, most engineering firms only complete a functional type of Depreciation Report. Any invasive testing requirements are then done as an additional fee for service.

In conclusion, the type of provider does not matter; a Strata Council usually will receive a Functional Depreciation Report. Therefore, unless the Strata Corporation wants invasive testing as part of the Depreciation Report, the type of Depreciation Report is usually immaterial to the choice of provider.

The Engineer is Mandatory.

The second part of the first question is, **Is the Engineer Mandatory?**

Engineers are essential for certain types of reserve planning assignments.

Invasive Testing

As discussed on the previous pages, you are ordering an Engineered Depreciation Report if there is invasive testing. And engineers are legally required to complete the work and sign off the paperwork.

Structural Concerns or Mould

Councils must consider remediation action for complexes with suspected or known structural or mould issues.

The two-storey separation of stucco allowing water ingress requires an Engineer.

If a concrete building envelope is damaged, it will cause cracks and spalling. This damage can allow seeds to take hold and start vegetation growth in walls and roofs as the moisture provides nutrients for the vegetation to take root. As the vegetation increases over time, the cracks will expand. As the vegetation size decreases, the moisture has a path to the interior of the building walls.

Water can damage and rust the metal attachments holding exposed windows, balcony railings, glass canopies and other fixtures. In extreme cases, moisture can corrode the metal rebar of concrete walls.

If a wood frame building envelope is damaged, this can allow moisture ingress, leading to mould and rot. Mould can create health issues, weakening the building on a structural level if not repaired. In that case, the support structure holding exposed windows, balcony railings, glass canopies and other fixtures can lose integrity.

This type of damage usually has consequences that planners cannot assess until well into the project's testing phase or as the covering is removed, making the costs unpredictable and unknown until the work is complete. This scope of work is more than a simple Depreciation Report.

From a financial planning point of view, structural repair costs are much more significant than simple renewal costs. Engineers should be relied upon for project management, especially if they have experience in this type of work.

In addition, legislation requires that an engineer approve restoration projects for mould or structural issues. As such, it is better to start with one to assist with costs and timing projections.

In conclusion, an engineering firm is mandatory in buildings where the council wants invasive testing or in a complex with known structural problems or mould requiring remediation.

When An Engineer is Recommended

Engineers or senior building technologists (10+ years of experience) collaborating with an engineer are recommended for high-rise or taller buildings with concrete or pre-engineered building envelopes.

The construction is complex, with specialized mechanical components like high-speed elevators, chillers, engineered window systems, etc. Analysis of these buildings is complicated because the technology constantly changes, and costs can vary per floor.

However, as discussed later in the chapter, a Team Approach may be more appropriate in many cases.

An Engineer is Not Required

This page answers the question. *When can I use a non-engineer provider?*

Just as engineers are required in some cases, experienced non-engineers can provide superior inspections for Functional Depreciation Reports at a more cost-effective price for the following property types:

Wood Frame

If you are in a wood-frame building or a brick building with a wood frame with no structural concerns or mould, the components and technology will be basic. The building envelope costs are typically stable on a floor-to-floor basis.

Townhome complexes are typically on slabs with asphalt shingle roofing. More opulent developments have clubhouses, roof decks and underground parking. These are easy to inspect and can be integrated within a report.

An apartment-type building is relatively easy to price out. Given the basic mechanical systems, including elevators and HVAC systems, engineers are usually not required.

A clubhouse can have more components than the rest of a complex. The reason is that the exterior envelope of the building, as well as the interior room finishings, and all the Furniture, Fixtures and Equipment (FF&E) or common Assets must be measured or counted and reviewed. As the cost of a Depreciation Report is usually based on how many components go into the report, it is easy to understand how the cost increases. Therefore, while the cost may be greater in a large amenity complex, it does not necessarily mean it is more complicated.

Industrial or Business Parks

These complexes tend to be wood-framed or concrete tilt-up construction with basic technology and mechanical components. Like wood-frame buildings, these are relatively easy to inspect and integrate within a report.

Bare Land

These developments have only a few features; however, the components tend to last a long time. But when they do break or need replacement, they are expensive. An experienced person without engineering training can cost out the roadway, services, and other components with good plans.

As we have already discussed, the key is the experience of the inspection staff, not their designations.

The Team Approach

Sometimes, using an engineer with a non-engineer provider best meets the needs of the Strata Corporation. This team approach is taking root in BC as engineers may be great at determining the replacement cost of a damaged exterior wall; they do not want to count patio lights, review furniture, or measure carpeting. This approach allows each team member to do what they do best.

This team approach occurs in three inspection scenarios.

The first scenario is when an envelope, structural or mould issue has been identified and a remediation plan has been prepared. The structural or mould damage will lead to a significant renovation or restoration program for the complex. Still, the damage is usually just on the exterior building envelope or the underground membrane, affecting only some items in the Depreciation Report.

The second scenario is when the Strata Corporation has a complex component, like geothermal heating or a chiller on the rooftop. A condition of the contract may require a supplementary engineer's report on that particular item.

The third scenario occurs when a significant component is nearing the end of its lifespan, and the provider recommends that a specialist be brought in. An example is when the roof or elevator is over 20 years of age, and a roofing inspector or elevator consultant joins the team.

Considering that a non-engineer provider can utilize the engineers' or specialists' costs and timing for renovation or restoration programs, many Strata Corporations are finding the most cost-effective solution is a cooperative approach in which the engineering firm concentrates on its area of specialization and a non-engineer provider completes the remainder of the report.

Added Value Specialists

The third question Strata Councils must ask is *When do I need a Specialist?*

Understanding the inspection staff and what expertise specialists will provide is essential. Specialists focus on one area and provide a supplementary report to the provider.

In most cases, reserve planning firms, engineering or not, may advertise these services but will seek specialists outside the firm. If there are any concerns, they need to be discussed with providers before signing contracts.

Thermographic Imaging Consultants

Thermographic imaging uses a specialized infrared camera to determine the conditions between the interior and the exterior walls without invasive testing. The scope of a typical Depreciation Report does not include thermographic imaging.

Imaging tools are available, but most Depreciation Report firm inspection staff are not qualified to interpret the results and, therefore, do not use them for liability reasons.

A certified professional should be the only one interpreting thermographic imaging. Certification is earned after rigorous training and proven experience in interpreting thermographic images.

Thermographic imaging is usually required if there are complaints of air leaks, drafts, cold exterior walls, or poor insulation.

Usually, air leaks or drafts are due to settling in the first decade of the building's life. Thermographic imaging will usually allow insulation failures or hidden misalignment due to settling to be discovered.

Cold walls on the building exterior are usually an indicator of poor insulation. Insulation can condense and settle, thinning out in specific locations or at the top of walls, and simply disappear. It aids in determining a failure of the insulation, water ingress, overheating of electrical components, or air leaks.

A Level 1 or 2 certified thermographer should be hired for an inspection before or during the Depreciation Report inspection if you have any of the above issues.

Roofing Inspectors

Depreciation Report inspectors are generalists who look at roofs for pooling, seam breakage, or bubbles indicating air gaps, among other issues. Roofing inspectors do a more comprehensive review of the above and tend to inspect items such as slopes that Depreciation Report inspectors do not measure.

Registered Roofing Observers (RRO) are experienced roofers who have received inspection training from the Roofing Contractors Association of BC (RCABC).

For this reason, insurers and warranty providers view RROs as physical analysis specialists needed for compliance with their policies while looking at reserve planners as roof inspection generalists with financial modelling and planning expertise.

Generally, roofs should be inspected after a new roof is installed, then every five years for the first 20 years, followed up with 3-year inspections as they get closer to the end of their lifespan.

If the roof is over 20 years of age, and there is no recent roofing inspection report, an RRO should do the report immediately before the Depreciation Report inspection.

Elevator Consultants

All buildings with elevators must have a licensed elevator contractor for maintenance. Buildings either have a hydraulic elevator (with the elevator room in the basement) or a traction elevator (with the elevator room on the roof). If an elevator breaks down, the cost to repair it will be high and cause access issues for the owners.

Depreciation Report providers do not evaluate elevators because only provincially licensed inspectors can assess an elevator's condition. Unless there is an additional report from an elevator consultant, it is dangerous for a provider to extend an elevator beyond its expected life. A provider can shorten the remaining lifespan if there is evidence of problems; however, the owners will have to contribute more money in a shorter time span to cover the replacement costs.

If the elevator is over 20 years old or jerking or stopping unexpectedly, an elevator consultant is recommended to do a condition assessment, estimated lifespan, and cost report before the Depreciation Report inspection.

Electrical Consultants

More insurers are reviewing buildings with electrical wiring, especially aluminum wiring and connections. As a known fire flashpoint, identification and potential removal are essential in reducing premiums. If the building was constructed between 1964 and 1984, the owners should have one of these one-time reports completed in conjunction with the inspection process.

The issue is that aluminum wiring is prone to losing shape and structure due to repeated temperature changes. If the wiring becomes structurally unstable, it can become a fire hazard. These hazards have been the subject of many insurance claims. Therefore, many insurers demand electrical inspection reports. If the inspection report reveals hot spots, the Strata Corporation must remove them.

Most wiring is removable without damaging the unit. However, when the wiring is behind walls and floors, the replacement cost may include wood framing, flooring, drywall or ceiling tiles, painting and maybe insulation. In that case, a renovation firm should coordinate the replacement project.

The other type of electrical report is the periodic inspection of the electrical panels for a building or groups of buildings for dust, damage, and connection problems. These can be a fire hazard, but more importantly, they can reduce electrical flow. A thermographic imaging consultant can do this.

It is recommended that owners arrange for this electrical report before the Depreciation Report inspection so the provider can include any costs resulting from the potential damage that is not visible.

Plumbing Consultants

As with electrical connections, insurers are concerned with piping, focusing on Poly-B (polybutylene). Poly-B is a flexible plastic plumbing piping commonly used between 1978-1995. Poly-B was popular for builders as it was much cheaper than copper piping. However, it has been the cause of significant leaks 10 to 15 years after installation. It has since been banned and has been the subject of many insurance claims. Many insurers are demanding its removal.

Pinhole leaks in the pipes usually cause water leaks. They are very damaging, especially in areas without visible water damage. A plumber should investigate leak repairs, but as the piping may be behind walls, floors or ceilings, the replacement costs may include wood framing, drywall or ceiling tiles, painting, and insulation. Plumbing inspection reports typically do not give a replacement cost. The restoration cost should be coordinated with a renovation firm.

A plan for identification and replacement is essential for insurance premium management. This type of plumbing review is a one-time report that a Strata Corporation should do before or in conjunction with the Depreciation Report inspection.

As with water leaks, a small replacement project in a wood-framed building is usually coordinated with a renovation firm. Replacement projects in concrete mid-rise to high-rise structures usually will require an engineer as part of the restoration team.

Community Water or Waste System Specialists

A community water system is a well or other non-municipal water source for development. Many of the water systems have testing facilities. In larger complexes, the system is tied to a community water treatment centre before being distributed to the properties.

A community waste system is a set of pumps to cisterns. The grey water is distributed to an industrial septic field. There also may be a treatment facility involved.

If no treatment or testing is required, the general rule is that a specialist report under the appropriate legislation for managing the well, community water, septage system or septic system would be necessary.

It is recommended that all developments with a water or wastewater testing or treatment centre involve a specialist to do a condition analysis, estimated lifespan and cost report before the inspection. As stated earlier, this would be within a chemical engineer's area of expertise.

Technical Specialists

A variety of other individuals may be used in a team approach that is not listed above but may contribute to the overall effectiveness of a Depreciation Report. As the property becomes more complex, some of these individuals may be recommended.

There are approximately 34,000 Strata Corporations in British Columbia, of which around 18,000 are outside the legislation as they have four or fewer units, meaning approximately 16,000 complexes must get Depreciation Reports.

With around 2,800 high-rises, around 18% of the complexes under this legislation are recommended to get an engineer or work within a Team.

The other 82% of developments have different options, including non-engineer providers, specialists, and a team approach with specialized engineers working together.

Readers can find a series of checklists summarizing the selection process on the following pages to assist decision-makers in finding the right provider for the right property type.

Question 1: Do I Need an Engineer?

First, determine if you require Invasive Testing (an Engineered Depreciation Report)

The first question Council members must determine is if an Engineered Depreciation Report is necessary due to invasive testing requirements.

Is Invasive Testing Required?	The building may require structural repair	Yes
	Mould is evident	Yes
	Walls have evidence of cracks or shifting	Yes
	Evidence of rot or moisture ingress exists	Yes

If Yes to any of the above, engage a Structural Engineer.

Second, determine if an Engineer is recommended.

Is an Engineer Recommended to the Building Complexity?	High-Rise	Yes
	Wood-frame townhome or low-rise apartment complex	No
	Industrial complex	No
	Bare Land	No

Even if you respond No to any of the above, a specialty Engineer may still be required, even when there is no invasive testing. Please review the checklist on the following page.

Question 2: Do I Need a Speciality Engineer?

Is a Structural Engineer required?	Do we want a structural evaluation of the envelope?	Yes
	Are we completing a warranty review? See the definition in the next chapter.	Yes
	Are we planning remodelling or additions to existing structures, or do we have issues relating to decks and patios?	Yes, but not part of the Depreciation Report.
	Are we planning for new safety or roof equipment, HVAC equipment or solar panels?	Yes
Is A Civil Engineer required?	Do we require cost estimates, documentation, or building code review due to planned remodelling or additions to existing structures, or do we have some issues relating to decks and patios?	Yes
	Do we require project management on a significant renewal project?	Yes, but not part of the Depreciation Report.
	Do we require project management on a significant renewal project?	Yes
Is a Mechanical Engineer required?	Do we have Complex Heating, Ventilation, and Air Conditioning (HVAC) units?	Yes
	Complex boilers, pumping systems and compressors?	Yes
	Any thoughts on re-piping the building or complex?	Yes
	Basic (HVAC) systems – Make Up Air units?	No
	Typical boilers, hot water tanks and expansion tanks?	No
Is an Electrical Engineer required?	Testing of loads in the building?	Yes
	Review of capacity for increasing loads for items like Electric Vehicle charges?	Yes
	Any thoughts on re-wiring the building or complex?	Yes
	Is thermographic imaging of electrical panels required?	No

Is A Chemical Engineer required?	Municipal Water and Municipal Sewage?	No
	Municipal Water and Septic Field?	No
	Municipal Water and Septage Tank system?	No
	Community well system?	Maybe, See specialists
	Community wastewater system?	Maybe, See specialists

If nothing above indicates an engineer is required, you can look for a Provider with an alternate designation.

If you need someone other than a Civil or Structural Engineer, a Provider with a Team Approach, as described earlier in the book, may be the best choice to meet the needs of the Strata Corporation at a more realistic cost.

Strata legislation does not spell out the role of Specialists, but they are key supporting players in many complexes' Depreciation Reports. Please review the checklist for common specialists on the following page.

Question 3: Is a Specialist Required?

The following Chart should Assist in determining if a Specialist is required to meet your needs.

Type of Specialist Required	Air leaks in buildings.	Thermographic Imaging
	Insulation - Cold walls in Winter / Sweating walls in Summer.	Thermographic Imaging
	Fear of water ingress.	Thermographic Imaging
	Roof over 20 years of age at the time of inspection.	RRO designated Inspector
	Elevator over 20 years of age at the time of inspection.	Elevator Inspector
	Elevator is jerking or stopping unexpectedly.	Elevator Inspector
	Building built between 1978-1995.	Poly-B Plumbing Report
	Building built between 1965-1984.	Aluminum wiring Electrical Report
	Community water system.	Person designated under provincial drinking water regulations
	Community water system with treatment facility.	Chemical engineer
	Community waste system.	Person designated under provincial sewerage regulations
	Community waste system with treatment facility.	Chemical engineer

The past two chapters focus on choosing a provider type. The following few chapters will assist the reader in identifying how to identify the best providers and overcome reoccurring common issues that I have identified in the past decade.

Chapter 5 – Reports Commonly Confused with Depreciation Reports

Sometimes, council members base their needs decisions on a misunderstanding of what should be included within a Depreciation Report or what can be used to replace a Depreciation Report on the assumption that they can save money.

Maintenance Manuals

Maintenance manuals contain information on operating, servicing, repairing, and decommissioning building devices, equipment, infrastructure, and utilities so their lifespans are maximized. Typically, the developer does these when a building is new, hoping that these manuals are periodically updated as modern technology is installed. It is recommended that these manuals be updated for high-rise buildings as building codes or operational recommendations change. These changes relate to elevators, HVAC, electrical, or plumbing standards.

As most technology is basic in wood-frame townhomes or low-rise multi-family buildings, many developments do not renew the manuals unless equipment is changed (replaced).

Maintenance manuals are not part of the legislation regarding the Depreciation Report and, therefore, are outside the typical report's scope.

Technical Reviews

Technical review means *"the application of scientific, engineering or other professional expertise to the facts to determine whether the activity for which a permit is requested meets the standards for issuing the permit under statute or rule."*

In other words, does the new component (replacement or repaired) meet the current building, electrical, plumbing, or other codes enforced today? Determining code requirements is typically outside the scope of a Depreciation Report. However, most experienced providers have an idea of what is not permitted.

Technical reviews are usually completed on only one component, like the heating system. Since there is no analysis of the other building components, it does not comply with the Depreciation Report legislation.

Electrical Vehicle Charging Stations (EV Ready Reports)

On April 6, 2023, the Government proposed significant changes to the Strata Property Act to make it easier for strata corporations and owners to install electric vehicle charging stations (EVCS). This was passed on May 11, 2023. This is an issue for Depreciation Reports as they include uncertainty in the planning.

Strata Corporations must plan for the needs of owners and residents. New Federal requirements require all new passenger car and truck sales to have zero emissions by 2035. In 2019, the province passed the Zero-Emission Vehicles Act, which aims for 10% of all new light-duty cars and trucks sold in B.C. to be zero emission by 2025. By 2040, they'll all need to be emission-free. As a result, B.C. legislators have legislation waiting to be enacted to create a "right-to-charge."

One way to make it easier for EV owners to force the Strata to undertake the expense of upgrading the electrical system and installing E.V. charging stations was to make the reports easy to get and lower the voting threshold from 75% to 50% for approval of the costs and changes to the property needed to install them. It must be remembered that only one request can trigger a requirement to get a report. Several planning reports may be undertaken before the electrical upgrading work is completed as votes fail and costs change.

Most people only see the charging station in a parking stall. However, this is just one part of a larger system with several parts, including multiple electrical and communication conduits, new transformers to accommodate increased power requirements, independent monitoring systems to account for the cost of individual power usage, visitor parking point of sales terminals, and so on. The installation of these E.V. stations can require substantial work and cost.

Strata Councils should ask the providers how this expense will be handled. Unless the Council notifies me that an EVCS report is planned, many providers will project that a report will be completed at a low expense year between 2024 and 2030, in keeping with legislation and vehicle sale targets.

With respect to the actual EV charging stations, I do not think that many Owners will vote to upgrade the entire electrical system at the cost of hundreds of thousands of dollars during the years 25-35 or 55-65 of a building's life, as this is a period of high expected costs, like replacement of roofs. Given the limited money most Strata Corporations have and the choice between new roofs or E.V. stations for the minority of occupants, I believe reaching the 50% threshold will be challenging in the next few years.

Councils should work with the provider to determine the best time to account for this one-time cost as the complex's demand for charging stations increases.

Given the above, these reports also do not comply with the Depreciation Report legislation.

EV Ready Reports should be completed before the Depreciation Report so the Owners can vote on the recommendations and incorporate the results into the report.

Electrical Planning Reports (EPRs)

This is a new type of mandatory report for strata corporations with 5 units or more. These reports relate to current and future EV charging infrastructure, heating, cooling, ventilation, and lighting systems. There is a December 31, 2026, deadline if the strata corporation is inside the Capital Regional District (Greater Victoria), the Fraser Valley Regional District, or the Metro Vancouver Regional District. Outside these areas, the deadline is December 31, 2028.

These reports must state the current capacity of the strata corporation's electrical system, a list of existing demands on the electrical system, a discussion of the current peak demand on and spare capacity of the electrical system, an estimate of the electrical capacity needed for any other anticipated future demands on the electrical system. Finally, it must include any steps the strata corporation could practically take to reduce the demands on the capacity of the electrical system, including upgrades or modifications, if any, to the electrical system that the strata corporation could practically undertake to increase the capacity of the electrical system and an estimate of the electrical capacity that would be made available if the strata corporation were to take steps to undertake upgrades or modifications referred to in the report.

Under the legislation, depending on the complexity of the buildings, the report must be completed by an electrical engineer, a registered applied science technologist, a construction electrician or an industrial electrician. Thus, they cannot be completed by the typical type of qualified Depreciation Report providers.

Electrical planning reports, like technical reviews, are usually completed on only one type of component (electrical system) and are one-time reports. They do not include costing, so the result is not reported in a Depreciation Report.

Given the above, these reports also do not comply with the Depreciation Report legislation.

If possible, this report should be completed before the Depreciation Report so the Owners can vote on the recommendations and the results incorporated into it.

Building Envelope Condition Assessment (BECA)

The building envelope is the outer shell that maintains a dry, heated, or cooled indoor environment and facilitates climate control. Building Envelope Condition Assessments (BECA) are designed to ensure that the building envelope (siding, roof, doors, windows, and balconies) does its job.

Building envelope inspections are extensive visual inspections of all exterior areas of the building and a comprehensive report. A BECA usually focuses on:

- The integrity of exterior surfaces.
- Moisture control.
- Ultraviolet protection
- A list of deficiencies.

These reports are out of the scope of the typical Depreciation Report for three main reasons:

First, there is invasive testing. As discussed in Chapter 4, this is outside the expected level of inspection that would be in a Functional Depreciation Report. This type of report would be at the level of expertise of a specialist (i.e., Building Envelope Specialist) or engineer.

Second, a building envelope inspection typically does not include more than 35% of the items in a Depreciation Report, as it only focuses on the building envelope. Interior finishings, amenities, and most electrical or mechanical components are outside the report's scope.

Finally, BECA reports are primarily used to review warranties or structural concerns. They are not useful as a financial planning tool, which is the legislated purpose of a Depreciation Report.

Warranty Reviews/Performance Audits

Warranty reviews are inspections to determine if a claim for poor workmanship or poor-quality materials is required. The warranty may be the new home warranty program, such as the 2/5/10 warranty in BC, or a specific item warranty (e.g., a new roof).

In BC, just before the warranty period for a group of issues terminates, an "end of warranty" inspection and report by an engineering consultant is undertaken, usually by a specialist (i.e., structural engineer).

As discussed in the book, predictability is a crucial feature of the Depreciation Report component selection. Warranty issues are based on replacing an item due to poor installation or products. As replacements or renewals under warranty are unpredictable, they cannot be planned. As such, these items are typically not included in a report.

Some believe providers should perform warranty reviews/performance audits simultaneously with the inspection. The assumption is that the engineer can make notes about the building and create a Depreciation Report.

This assumption is incorrect.

Unlike building envelope inspections, warranty reviews cover most of the important items in a building, but not simultaneously. Assessments are timed when there is a problem or just before the end of the warranty period. Reviews are limited to a specific item or group of related items, which may happen a few times at the beginning of the building's lifespan or after an item is replaced.

For example, while a roofing inspector may review the roof nine years after installation, this inspector will not do the carpeting simultaneously. Some items, like furniture, may not show in warranty reviews but will be in a reserve planning document.

Another important distinction is that warranty reviews can lead to litigation, so invasive or more rigorous testing may be required. As discussed earlier, this is not part of the expected level of inspection in a Depreciation Report.

Suppose you want the engineer to simultaneously provide the Depreciation Report and a more in-depth warranty review/performance audit on a specific item or related group of items. In that case, there would be a substantial additional fee.

In summary, Strata Councils should complete Depreciation Reports separately from other reports.

Chapter 6 – Property Managers and Suppliers

Strata Corporations have three management options: self-administered, self-administered with financial support, and professional management, where the Council has a licensed Property Manager to assist them.

Self-administrated Stratas are usually smaller developments in which the Council members oversee all operations, including choosing suppliers.

In a self-administered complex, the Strata Council should look for providers by looking at websites with memberships in organizations such as CHOA (Condominium Homeowners Association) and PAMA (Property Agents and Managers Association), as well as friends who live in other developments. This book is also a guide.

Self-administrated with financial support are developments that have financial administration assistance from the accounting department of a property management firm, but otherwise are on their own. Assistance with choosing suppliers is usually outside the service contract or will be an additional fee.

Professional management is where the Council has a licensed Property Manager to assist them.

Despite the type of management, if the Strata has the assistance of a property manager, the Council needs to be aware of some issues.

Property managers are employees of management companies and are bound by the company's policies. Therefore, councils need to ensure corporate policy does not limit their choice of providers.

"Approved" or "Preferred" Suppliers

Some property managers have a corporate policy to only recommend names from their "approved supplier" or their "preferred supplier" list. These are suppliers that the property management firm has vetted in some manner.

Depreciation Reports are valuable documents that lenders, insurers, and purchasers will examine. Council should make sure they are fully informed, as a poorly written report will remain around for five years.

I recommend Councils insist that property managers provide a list of at least three Depreciation Report providers that meet their needs, including providing samples. If the property management firm does not have three choices, it is the Council's responsibility to look for alternative Depreciation Report providers outside the property manager's "approved/preferred" list.

If you have heard good things about another provider, just ask your property manager for a proposal. Outside of quality issues, there are many reasons why property management firms may not have a name on their list, from personality disagreements to the policy on the number of a type of supplier on the list.

"Engineers Only" Suppliers

Some property management firms only want engineers to do Depreciation Reports, but as I have outlined in this book, this may be overkill for the needs of the Strata Corporation.

If you are in a high-rise, I would expect all the suppliers on the list to be engineers or a mix of engineers and non-engineers within a single team, as previously discussed.

Non-engineers are qualified if you are in a bare land development, industrial strata, townhome, or low-rise building. If the property manager provides only engineering firm names, **you should ask why.**

Some property management firms have separate lists for engineers, appraisers, and other specialists but no specific Depreciation Report provider category.

This lack of categorization is a disservice to their clients, the Strata Corporations. Depreciation Reports require special skills, knowledge, and experience that others in the same profession may not have. If this is the case with your property management firm, **you should ask why there is no list of professional Depreciation Report specialists.**

Whether the potential provider is on the property management list or not, an engineer or not, the Council has a duty to complete its research. The best tool for reviewing a potential supplier is to read a sample report.

Chapter 7 – Conflicts of Interest

Conflicts of interest occur when a provider may have a possible or actual vested interest. A vested interest is someone having or wanting to have a continuing interest in the complex. Many of the depreciation reports I reviewed over the past decade have such conflicts of interest.

As mentioned in the introduction, professional reserve planning organizations got together in the 1990s in the USA, partially due to ethical dilemmas. The current strata legislation does not have conflict restrictions. Unfortunately, until the ethical issues are resolved in BC, strata councils must be the gatekeepers.

Some conflicts of interest are common sense. Nobody who owns, occupies or leases a strata lot should do the Depreciation Report in the same complex.

Nobody connected to the current property management firm, or their family should be engaged. The fear is that the property management firm will use undue influence to make the report look better than the actual state.

Likewise, nobody connected to another property management firm should be used. This information may be used for internal building comparison statistics or give them inside knowledge to allow them to offer to take over building management.

One concern is Appraisers with a real estate license. Councils should avoid realtors and anyone related to realtors completing a Depreciation Report for their complex. Even a proposal may allow them inside knowledge about the building and additional contacts for marketing. Considering that the Depreciation Report fee is far below the Realtor's commission for one sale, it is impossible to be confident that the Depreciation Report would be unbiased.

The truth is many appraisers hold active real estate or property management licenses to gain better or cheaper access to real estate data. While many are not really active, if concerned, ask another realtor who can check the local real estate board for the number of transactions the person in question may have had in the past year. The Council may want to look to another provider if they have done a few deals in the past year.

Another significant issue is CRPs or Engineers who are also contractors, where they can have inside knowledge of upcoming work.

Knowing when a building will require work and whom to contact is invaluable for the contractor. They will know when to contact the Strata Council. By estimating the projected time and cost for the Depreciation Report, the contractor can create a proposal when the work is required, just under the report's estimate, meaning it will most likely be approved. If the work is small or the strata is small, it has a good chance of being the sole bid or single-sourced contract.

Owners do not know if the contracting firm's or the complex's financial interest is reflected in the report. I am always wary of people who state they can do the report and fix anything outstanding.

Other contractors, even those with a better reputation or lower price, may not get a chance to bid. And if they do, they are disabled without knowing what's in the report.

I occasionally hear of these conflicts being disregarded because the provider has the lowest price. However, councils that knowingly sign a contract, aware of the possible conflict of interest, open themselves to favouritism and potential Civil Resolution Tribunal (CRT) claims. Whoever wins at the CRT does not matter; the resources spent will be greater than any savings.

The exception to this rule is when the council believes there is an engineering issue within the complex and brings in an engineer. In other words, an Engineered Depreciation Report is being completed.

Recently, I ran into a situation where a property management firm offered to pay for the Depreciation Reports of new clients. This practice is dangerous as it interferes with the client relationship between the Strata Corporation and the provider.

The problem arises when one party, such as the insurer or the property manager, offers to pay for the report for a new client. They decide who the provider is, sign the contract, and pay for the report. The Strata Corporation did not order or pay, so they are not the client. As a result, legally, the provider must take directions from the insurer or property manager who ordered it. This may not align with the Strata Corporation's interests.

Property managers should not advise Strata Corporations to use those firms with an actual or potential conflict of interest. However, council members ultimately make the decisions and must ensure the recommended providers have no vested interest. If you are unhappy with the property manager's choices, search for another option and tell the property management firm why you feel there is a conflict issue.

Most professional providers understand conflicts of interest issues and have a clause or statement in their proposal covering them. When a Strata Council may have concerns or no statement, you can use a letter like the one on the following page.

JEREMY BRAMWELL, AACI, P.APP, RI

Sample Letter to Remove Potential Conflicts

July 15, 2024

Professional Reserve Planning Group
456 Anywhere Road
Surrey, BC V9V 9V9

RE: Depreciation Report for Strata Corporation ABC123 (The Best Building)

Dear Mr. Provider:

Regarding your proposal for a Depreciation Report at the above property, we need to confirm that there are no conflicts of interest. Please read, sign, and return this document before September 5, 2024, so we can make an informed decision. If you cannot sign the document, please email strata@gmail.com by August 31, 2024.

As a representative of the above firm, I, the undersigned, state that the following is correct.

1. No company ownership or management, direct family members, or employees of the firm own, lease, or occupy a unit in the complex.
2. None of the company ownership or management, their direct family members, or employees of the firm is a licensed Property Manager or Realtor.
3. None of the company owners, management, their direct family members, or employees are invested in, employed by, or manage a contracting business where they can know about upcoming work. An exception is an engineering firm, given engineers can complete only some work required under the law or insurance provisions.
4. As a provider, you will have access to information that is not publicly available. The report will not be used as an invitation to bid for work discussed in the report. The report will not have any unsolicited bids for work indicated in the report, attached to the report, in the same envelope or email that copies of the report are sent or forwarded.
5. No information collected may be given, sold, or transmitted to another party outside your firm for free or any benefit.
6. (OPTIONAL) You agree not to provide bids for work in the report until after the following Depreciation Report is available.

It is understood that a violation of the agreement will be deemed a breach of the contract, with a full refund of the fee paid.

Chapter 8 – The Fee Is Not Everything

Over the years, I have heard Strata Councils say they want the cheapest option. It is easy to focus on the fee and the fee alone, but there are other things to consider. None of the owners want to overpay. Everyone should focus on getting the best value for the money.

One issue not often discussed is the provider's understanding of the legal side of the report.

A good start is to enquire about legislation regarding Depreciation Reports. Providers should understand the legal issues related to openings (doors, windows, and skylights) and developer-installed amenities. AACI and CRP-designated providers tend to have superior knowledge as this is part of their training. This knowledge gives them an edge over engineers and people with more technical backgrounds in particular situations.

If you have shared amenities, sectioned buildings, developments with air parcel agreements or developer-installed amenities, ask them how these will be treated in the report or if a supplementary report will be required. If you disagree, choose another firm. It does not matter if you are correct; the conflict will be a problem for all parties.

Next, council members should consider a specialist's costs for a supplementary report. Some providers will include it if they know the council wants to engage one in the proposal stage. After the report is in progress, inclusion will be much more expensive and time-consuming.

Finally, those ordering the reports need to understand what is included in the fee and the services they will receive. I have seen many inclusive contracts with extra costs, such as:

- Travel charges.
- Additional inspection charges, if required.
- Draft meeting charges.
- Change charges if the report must be changed.
- Printed copy charges.
- Server storage charges.
- AGM/SGM attendance fees.

Not all the above fees are unwarranted, but the council needs to know them before signing the contract.

One issue not usually discussed is the issue of changes. If data is given to the provider and they complete a report based on that information, then they find out the data is incorrect; it is very reasonable to understand that the provider will charge an additional fee for these changes. This is not the same as in a Draft meeting where the goal is to clarify the data and work to a mutually acceptable conclusion. This is why completing the providers' questionnaire, discussed in Chapter 13, must be done as diligently as possible.

Comparing the report costs, with and without additional services, is essential. However, the most important thing is to ensure that the provider meets your needs for inspecting the development carefully so they can recommend a realistic funding model.

Chapter 9 – When to Order the Report

Strata Councils need to understand when to order the Depreciation Report. The legal requirements and the typical service timelines set out when to order the report.

Since 2011, Depreciation Reports were to be ordered every three years. Until 2024, this requirement could be continually deferred for up to 18 months with a 75% vote at an AGM. This has led to an estimated 80% of Stratas having old or no reports.

Under the new regulations, if the Strata completed a Depreciation Report effective January 1, 2021, or later, you have 5 years to obtain a current Depreciation Report.

Suppose your complex has never ordered a report or has a report with an effective date in 2020 or before. In that case, the Strata Council must get a Depreciation Report by July 1, 2026, if it is located in the Lower Mainland (Metro Vancouver or Fraser Valley regional districts) or the Capital Regional District (excluding the Gulf Islands and all other islands).

The deadline is July 1, 2027, everywhere else in BC.

For new complexes, that is, Strata Corporations registered after July 1, 2024, the report must be completed by the second AGM.

Outside these legal requirements, there are practical considerations. A Depreciation Report has several steps before it is delivered in its final form.

First, the Property Manager or Council must order the proposal for the Council to review. Once the Council reviews the proposal, it must enter the contract and send the deposit (retainer) to the provider. Depending on the Council and the property management firm's payment processing timing, this can take 14 to 60 days. Most providers do not start until the management firm has issued a work order or a deposit cheque.

The second step is to collect documents and analyze them. This process can take a few days for a knowledgeable and proactive council or as long as a few months for those who grudgingly provide data in drips and drabs. The following section has an entire chapter on this.

The next step is the inspection process, which involves collecting data on-site so the provider can complete the report. The two items that determine the timing of the inspection date are the availability of inspection staff and the assistance of the strata council during the inspection. Coordinating inspection timing with a specialist can be an issue. The lack of a strata representative for the inspection also commonly delays the inspection date.

Sometimes, the inspection process gets extended for reasons unrelated to the strata council. There can be weather issues that do not make inspection possible, especially in Northern BC. Sometimes, inspection staff will have to do several inspections on the same day, slowing production time as the reports are generated. Specialists can slow the report's completion as providers and councils wait for their analysis. Sometimes, staffing issues at the provider, such as sick staff or a member who is no longer with the firm, stretch workflows.

One of the most time-consuming parts of the process is waiting for the Council to approve a date for a draft report meeting. The final copy is sent after the draft report is reviewed and corrections are made. Many contracts have clauses that state the report will be finalized within 30 days if no draft meeting is held, yet some councils are trying to increase this time by months.

Over the past decade, I have noticed that clients (councils) typically fall into three groups: Proactive, Hesitant and Turtles.

The Proactive group has all the documents ready, has prepared for the inspection, and expects the report to be completed as soon as possible.

The Hesitant group collects the documents when asked, sometimes repeatedly. Arranging the inspection takes time, and the Council expects the report when it arrives.

The data collection phase for Turtles takes forever, so nobody from the Strata is available for the inspection, and they do not care when the report comes, if ever.

These are the timelines that each group usually falls into.

	Proactive	Hesitant	Turtles
Contracting the Provider	2-3 Weeks	4-6 Weeks	7-10 Weeks
Collecting Documents	1-3 Weeks	4-10 Weeks	Over 10 Weeks
Inspection	2-3 Weeks	4-6 Weeks	7-10 Weeks
Draft Meeting	1-2 Weeks	3-5 Weeks	6-8 Weeks
Total	6-11 Weeks	15-27 Weeks	30-48 Weeks

The first day of the fiscal year is always the effective date of a Depreciation Report.

Under the legislation, a new report is required every five years. Assuming your Depreciation Report is completed with an effective date of March 1, 2024, the following report must have an effective date of March 1, 2029.

Before the change in the legislation, if a large group of owners failed to meet the threshold level to defer a Depreciation Report, they would block it on the budget.

Now, the Depreciation Report expense is like the insurance expense: it is just a matter of choosing a provider and putting the amount in the budget.

Given the above chart and the fact that the Depreciation Report needs to be obtained by the fifth anniversary (2029), Strata Corporation should order it at the fourth-year AGM (2028) for delivery next year.

Regardless of the type of client, if ordered after the fourth-year AGM, a reasonable provider should be able to get the report to the Council for the financial planning for the fifth-year (2029) budget.

When Strata Corporation authorizes the Depreciation Report at the fifth-year AGM, all the current-year financial budgets are complete and approved at the same AGM by the time the report is completed. The report would be backdated, so technically, it would follow the Strata Property Act, but as its purpose is financial planning, it loses some of its value.

In summary, ordering the Depreciation Report at the fourth-year AGM allows the Owners to get the most value from the report.

Chapter 10 – Proposal Review Analysis

The last step is to review the proposals.

The Depreciation Report Provider Comparison System following this chapter is suitable for engineering and non-engineering firms, from bare land developments to the tallest high-rises. The following pages have a recommended points guide and summary chart for comparing providers.

Most qualified firms have a quote system on the website or can respond to an email request if they know the strata plan number.

Some firms will allow a pre-contract council interview. This meeting is typically done remotely for 5-15 minutes during the workday at a predetermined time. Part of the interview should cover the writer's understanding of the strata legislation, especially if you have a complex with different types, shared amenities, sections, or air parcel agreements. Evening appointments are usually kept for draft meetings with clients.

A sample report should be available for any proposal. It is nice to have a sample report that matches your property type. You should expect a bare land sample if you are in a bare land development. However, the stock sample in many firms is an apartment building, and the style and contents will be similar. Within the proposal or the sample, there should be some indication of the provider's Depreciation Report standards.

Choosing your type of provider is based on the information in chapters three, four and five. The following four chapters are designed to assist the Strata Council in dealing with common issues that need to be considered as they decide on the best providers for their development.

Good luck with choosing a provider.

Depreciation Report Provider Comparison System

\multicolumn{3}{c}{The Most Important Consideration Is to Find Someone Who Is Qualified}		
Category:	Possible responses	Points per response
Designation(s):	Is the designation of the person signing the Depreciation Report listed in the Legislation?	
	Yes	Next Question
	No	Remove name
Conflicts of Interest:	Is there an actual or possible Conflict of Interest?	
	Yes	Remove name
	No	Next Question
Insurance Coverage (Errors & Omissions):	The legislation may not require providers to have E&O insurance, but you should.	
	Yes	4 points
	No	0 point
Recommendations:	Recommendations / Testimonials are helpful to seek out – Maximum of eight (8) points.	
	Recommended by a Property Manager	4 points
	If the Property Manager has no opinion	2 points
	If the Property Manager has a negative view based on experience	0 point
	Recommended by an Owner in a letter	4 points
	If no Owner testimonial is provided	0 points
Pre-contract Interview:	Council members find it particularly useful to have the person who will be drafting the report (not the salesperson) present their proposals so that they can evaluate their experience and skills.	
	Depreciation Report writers are available for an interview	2 points
	If not available	0 points
Construction Background Experience:	The longer the inspection staff have been involved in residential or commercial construction, renovations, or inspections, the more accurate and realistic the Depreciation Report's physical analysis of the complex will be.	
	Ten or more years	4 points
	5 to 10 years	2 points
	Less than five years	1 point
	No construction experience	0 point

The Most Important Consideration Is to Find Someone Who Is Qualified		
Category:	Possible responses	Points per response
Strata /Condominium Legislation Understanding:	Council members should also seek providers who understand the strata legislation.	
	Understands the legislation and how it relates to your complex	4 points
	Incomplete understanding of the Act and how it relates to your complex	0 point
Sample of Work:	Reviewing a Depreciation Report sample allows you to verify the content and the format of the report.	
	If a work sample is available for your property type	4 points
	If a work sample is available	2 points
	If a work sample is not available	0 point
Specific Depreciation Report Standards:	All owners should have a Standards Based report. All providers should identify the Depreciation Reports standards being utilized, and where they can be found.	
	If the provider lists the specific Depreciation Reports standards used	4 points
	If the specific Depreciation Reports standards used is not listed or there are none	0 point

While the Fee is not Everything, understanding the Contract is essential.		
Category:	Possible responses	Points per response
Fee:	The overall cost for the services provided is determined to be the fee, usually before taxes.	
	Lowest fee	4 points
	Second lowest fee	3 points
	Highest fee	1 point
Specialists Fees:	If the provider recommends Engineers or Specialists as part of their services, is the supplementary fee separated?	
	Yes	4 points
	No	2 points
Disbursements:	These additional costs for travel, getting plans etc., without approval.	
	Lowest disbursements	4 points
	Second lowest disbursements	3 points
	Highest disbursements	2 points
	Disbursements are not discussed	0 point
Draft Depreciation Report Meeting:	Meeting with the writer to discuss the working copy (draft copy) ensures that the Depreciation Report will be accurate.	
	If the draft meeting is included in the fee	4 points
	If a draft meeting requires an additional disbursement	2 points
	If a draft meeting is not available	Remove the name
Additional Meetings:	Strata councils sometimes ask the writer to attend their Annual General Meeting. What is the cost?	
	Lowest cost to attend	4 points
	Second lowest cost	3 points
	Highest additional cost	2 points
	Not mentioned or available	0 points

Depreciation Report Provider Comparison Chart					
FIRMS PROVIDING PROPOSALS		**Provider # 1**	**Provider # 2**	**Provider # 3**	**Example**
					ABC Co.
		Score Below	**Score Below**	**Score Below**	
Report Writer Designation(s)					YES
Conflicts of Interest:					NO
Insurance Coverage (E & O):					4
Recommendations (Maximum 8 points):	Property Manager				4
	Owners Letter(s)				2
Pre-contract Interview:					2
Construction Experience:					4
Condo Legislation Understanding:					4
Sample of Work:					4
Specific Report Standards:					4
EXPERIENCE TOTAL:					**28**
Fee:					4
Specialists Options and Fees:					4
Disbursements:					3
Draft Discussion Meeting:					4
Additional Meetings:					4
Hard Copies of the Report:					2
Doing the Insurance Appraisal at the Same Time:					4
Annual Updates:					3
Fixed Renewal Fee:					4
VALUE TOTAL:					**32**
TOTALS					**60**
Maximum 66 Points					

Section Two

Physical Analysis

Chapter 11 – The Component Inventory

The goal of the physical analysis is to create the Component Inventory.

The Component Inventory is the task of selecting and quantifying reserve components. The inventory lists all the major components and assets the Strata Corporation is responsible for maintaining, such as exterior walls, roofing, hallways, elevators, amenity rooms, and parking.

Typically, a preliminary inventory is completed before the inspection based on the data provided to the provider. This task can be accomplished through on-site visual observations, a review of Strata Corporation design and organizational documents, a review of established Strata Corporation precedents, and a discussion with appropriate Strata Corporation representative(s).

A complete inventory is critical as it is the only way a reader can validate the information in the report. It is also key for proper financial modelling and benchmarking. Once the on-site inspection is complete, the inventory is finalized.

Reports can be easier to understand if the information is listed beside each component in the report. However, some providers just list them in a summary format. This terminology is used industry-wide.

Year of Acquisition: The year installed or when it was last replaced.

Expected Lifespan: The estimated time, in years, that a reserve component can be expected to serve its intended function if properly maintained and constructed in its present application or installation.

Effective Age: The chronological age is the actual age of the component. The effective age is the age based on the condition of the component.

When a component has not been taken care of, the provider will increase the effective age. This means the replacement must be replaced sooner and funded earlier, which will result in higher annual contributions. This is why properly maintaining all the building components will save money in the long term.

The good news is that when a component is well taken care of, it will last longer, decreasing the effective age.

Remaining Lifespan: The estimated time, in years, that a reserve component can be expected to continue to serve its intended function. The Expected Lifespan minus the Effective Age.

Unit Quantity: This is the quantity of a specific component in the complex. It may be on a per-unit basis (i.e., number of square feet, linear feet, or unit counts) for the specific items.

Unit of Measurement: The component's unit of measurement, such as the number of square feet, linear feet, or unit counts.

We have noticed some issues that can affect reliability in some other reports.

I have seen the same problem regarding lifespan calculations in the last few years. Some providers put the anticipated lifespan or effective age in a range, say, 25-30 years. For financial analysis purposes, it must be represented as a single number. If there is a range, the council should ask the provider to provide the number they used and why.

I also see providers not including per-unit quantities in the component summary.

In my opinion, these practices are being done for two reasons.

The first is liability reasons. If the owners cannot verify the data, how can they ask for changes to correct it?

The second reason for not including quantities is to incentivize clients not to change providers. When ordering an updated report, clients are typically given a discount over the cost of the initial report because some of the work is complete. If the owners want to move to another firm, they must incur the cost of a "first" report again. I believe some providers leave these numbers out to provide an economic reason for clients to return.

As we go through this section of the book, the reader should understand how providers collect the information and then determine if the components or assets belong in the component inventory of the Depreciation Report.

Below is a typical component summary that a reader can expect in a Benchmark Schedule, as discussed in Chapter 20. The following page is a checklist so the reader can check their provider's report for the issues discussed above.

RESERVE COMPONENTS	YEAR OF ACQUISITION	EXPECTED LIFESPAN	EFFECTIVE AGE	REMAINING LIFESPAN	UNIT QUANTITY	UNIT MEASURE
Structural and Architectural						
1 Concrete Slab Foundation	1988	70	33	37	1	allowance
2 Vinyl Siding	1988	50	33	17	14228	square feet
3 Structural Wood Posts - Basic	1988	50	33	17	13	posts
4 Attached Service Room	1988	70	33	37	1	allowance
5 Window Assemblies	1988	35	34	1	78	windows
6 Window Assemblies (Large)	1988	35	34	1	10	windows
7 Metal Townhome Entrance Doors	2012	40	9	31	20	doors
8 Sliding Doors	2019	35	2	33	14	doors
9 Exterior Painting and Stain	2019	10	2	8	2500	square feet
10 Caulking and Waterproofing	2009	12	11	1	2600	linear feet
11 Exterior Powerwashing	2020	10	1	9	14500	square feet
12 Single Garage Door	1988	25	20	5	10	doors
Roofing						
13 Chimney Caps	2017	25	4	21	16	caps and/or chases
14 Asphalt Shingle	2017	25	4	21	14847	square feet
15 Skylights (20 X 46 inches)	2017	25	4	21	9	skylights
16 Wood Fascia	2001	25	20	5	1982	linear feet
17 Gutters and Downspouts	1996	25	20	5	1082	linear feet
18 Aluminum Soffits	1988	40	30	10	4378	square feet
Electrical Systems						
19 Cluster Subdivision Distribution System	2004	70	17	53	10	allowances (Per SL)
20 GFCI Outlets	1988	25	20	5	20	outlets
21 Exterior Lights and Outlets	2012	25	9	16	40	lights
Mechanical Systems						
22 Domestic Water Distribution Systems - Cluster	1988	70	35	35	2	allowances (Per SL)
23 Buried Sanitary and Storm Drainage System	1988	70	35	35	2	allowances
24 Natural Gas Fireplace Exhaust Fan	2000	25	17	8	4	units
Amenities						
25 Garage Interiors	1988	60	30	30	1	allowance
Site Improvements						
26 Exterior Paths and Patios	1988	50	33	17	2235	square feet
27 Concrete Driveways	1988	70	33	37	4900	square feet
28 Cedar Fencing Replacement	2005	24	16	8	544	linear feet
29 Cedar Fencing Restaining	2005	8	6	2	3264	square feet
30 Wood Fencing Replacement	2005	24	17	7	210	linear feet
31 Wood Fencing Repainting	2020	8	1	7	1260	square feet
32 Landscaping	2018	6	3	3	13418	square feet
33 Wood Trellis	2012	25	9	16	100	linear feet
Consultant Report						
34 Depreciation Report Renewal	2021	3	0	3	1	report
TOTAL RESERVES						

Component Inventory Checklist			
√	Column	Note or Comments in Report if not shown in Component Inventory
☐	Year of Acquisition	
☐	Expected Lifespan	
☐	Effective Age	
☐	Remaining Lifespan	
☐	Unit Quantity	
☐	Unit of Measurement	

NOTES:

Chapter 12 – Collecting Documents

Depreciation Report providers are more efficient when they collect documents for analysis before a site inspection. Below is a list of the required documentation and why they are reviewed. At the end of the chapter, the three special situations of sectioned buildings, shared amenities, and air space parcels (ASP) are discussed in detail.

Documents

1. Legal Documents
2. Provider Questionnaire
3. Financial Documents
4. Building Plans
5. Maintenance Documents
6. Consulting Reports

Legal Documents

Strata Plan (the Legal Plan) - Inspectors use Strata Plans to determine Common Property (CP) or Limited Common Property (LCP), which is the common area or the physical space of the property that the report must cover. If there are no building plans, providers can use the strata plans for measuring hallways, roof coverage and the exterior area. However, these plans rarely indicate height.

Strata plans will also display phases. A phase is a portion of a development constructed in a different period, meaning the replacement year for later phases may differ from earlier phases. Phases will be discussed more in Chapter 14.

Current Bylaws - These provide for the administration of the Strata Corporation and the control, management, maintenance, use and enjoyment of the strata lots, common property, and common assets of the Strata Corporation. Strata Corporations may create bylaws that could give an owner financial responsibility instead of the development, or vice versa. Providers must review them.

Rules govern the common property and assets' use, safety, and condition. Rules cannot govern the use of strata lots; only bylaws can do this. Rules should not impact a Depreciation Report and, therefore, are usually not required.

Council Meeting Minutes and AGM/SGM Notices and Minutes - These documents provide a wealth of knowledge about what is happening in a complex and the specific areas that need attention. The minutes and notices should cover at least the last three years or the period since the previous report.

The following legal documents should be included, if applicable.

Alteration Agreement Summary - Alteration agreements occur when an owner takes responsibility for an attachment to the building envelope or something they have changed that is the Strata Corporation's responsibility. This list includes owners replacing common or limited common property like doors or windows at their costs, for which they assume liability for damage when installed or later from poor quality installation. Agreements are also encouraged when items like satellite dish antennas or patio covers are attached to the building envelope. A one-line summary page with the unit number, the date the installer completed the work, and a description of the work is required.

Lawsuits or Arbitration Decisions – These are decisions where a court or tribunal has decided that the responsibility of replacing or maintaining an asset or building component belongs to the Strata Corporation or the Owner. A typical example is when a dispute occurs regarding a fence.

Leases or Licenses for Equipment or Services - Sometimes, developments have rented equipment or have service agreements that include replacing assets if they break down during the service life. This document needs to be reviewed to account for any potential replacement expense.

Third-Party Use Agreements - Common areas, such as a commercial lobby or parking area, can be leased out long-term to non-owners. These leases need to be reviewed for revenue or cost implications.

Provider Questionnaire

Council Survey - All providers are trained to ask questions on-site during the inspection. However, questions are occasionally forgotten during the inspection when an unexpected response in an earlier matter comes up. Another frequent problem is when the strata representative showing the property does not know the complete history.

Experienced providers will ask the property management firm or the council members to gather past information and outline their future goals within a survey. Then, the provider can elicit more detailed information at the inspection if the survey information and the visual indicators during the site inspection do not match.

One of the most significant issues we have encountered is the council delaying the survey when they do not have all the information. The goal is to get as much information as possible from that council. Providers will understand if it is incomplete.

Problems occur when the council returns incorrect or undisclosed information and then suddenly remembers everything at the Draft meeting. I recommend that councils complete as much as possible and email any conflicting information back to the provider before the draft meeting.

Financial Documents

Three (3) Years of CRF Contributions and Interest Income

Depreciation Report providers need to know the history of CRF contributions to incorporate the current funding level into the report or recommend a change.

Interest income allows the calculation of the Interest Income Rate (IIR). The IIR is the average interest earned in the CRF account between low-interest income from the cash balance and higher returns from investments, like GICs. It is expressed as a percentage.

The three years relate to the period that is most relevant to a Depreciation Report. If more years are available since the last report, this will provide some more support, but it is not critical.

Normally we would expect this information to be separated on the financial documents provided to the owners with the AGM notices.

Three (3) Years of Fiscal Year-End Financial Statements

These financial statements are required to understand the past few years of spending. Often, providers find CRF items being spent from the operating fund, and the allocation needs correction.

The only financial documents usually required are those attached to the AGM notices sent to all owners or those attached to the past AGM minutes. These documents include the current income statement, expenditures, balance sheet, and budget.

Invoices and the general ledger are not required as they only lengthen the writer's document review time. After all, it is not an audit that is being conducted.

However, there are exceptions. For example, if work is significant, defined as 50% of the operating budget or greater, or the work is in progress, a copy of the invoice or contract is required for a more accurate report.

Most providers will also ask for quotes received for upcoming work.

Building Plans

The collection of plans is the most challenging function for providers. It can also be the greatest point of frustration and delay in the process.

Providers understand that the older the complex, the less likely the development will have these drawings.

The first question councils ask providers is, "do I need the plans?"

The answer lies between the age and complexity of the development.

Before I answer that question further, there is a truth that all strata councils need to understand. All Strata Corporations should have a complete set of plans, hopefully electronically or on paper. These drawings are required for all tradespeople, especially as the development gets older and major renovations are needed.

We all assume that the municipal halls will have a set in their archives, but more than a decade of experience has shown me this is not always a good bet. British Columbia is full of stories of village hall flooding (Sicamous) or storage building roof collapses in a snowstorm (Victoria). Strata Corporations that have ordered their own copy may save thousands of dollars if the council must replace them for major future work.

So, who should get the plans?

If the provider takes on the responsibility of getting the plans, they will charge for waiting at the city hall. Knowing that the council will need the plans later, the provider usually orders them all at the municipal hall. If the provider reviews the plans to find the ones he needs, the time charges can be more than the money saved by not ordering a few extra pages of plans. Ordering plans can be a few hundred to a thousand dollars, depending on the complexity and age of the building. This expense has led to frustration as it was a cost that the strata council was not expecting, or the council feels the provider should absorb the additional cost.

If a strata council member takes on the responsibility of getting the plans, they will need the written authorization of the council. The council members usually order the plans when they can, which may be weeks away. This council member may feel pressure from other council members if they have not dealt with city hall by the next meeting, potentially leading to resentment and frustration. Usually, the council members will not know which documents the provider needs, so they will order what pages they think are needed or all the plans.

We have heard that the Property Manager is sometimes asked to get the plans. To be fair, this is outside their scope of work and a waste of their time and expertise.

If the council decides they need a complete set of plans, what should they expect?

Below is a list of common types of drawings with a summary of their importance.

General Sheets: (G Series) These sheets usually begin the construction documents set. The general drawings include the cover page, building and zoning code analysis, life safety plans, and accessibility and sustainability standards, if required.

These sheets summarise information that can be very important to the provider.

Civil Engineering Sheets: (CE Series) These drawings include the Civil Engineer's notes, the grading and utilities plans, and other details.

These provide minimal data to the provider.

Architectural Sheets: (A Series) The architectural drawings graphically communicate (in plan, section, elevation, and details) the architectural components of the building design. Architects are most familiar with these drawing types, but there are similarities among all disciplines.

Architectural plans allow the most accurate measurements of building components. The older the complex, the less likely the development will have them. However, most municipal halls will have a set in their archives.

Structural Sheets: (S Series) The licensed Structural Engineer's drawings provide structural plans, calculations, and details - from an entire level's beam system to the detailed connection between structural elements. Detailed drawings and calculations for each type of structural system in the project are required.

Structural plans are usually irrelevant in smaller complexes but increase in importance in larger developments.

Plumbing Sheets: (A or M Series) The plumbing drawings will show all inbound and outbound water supply locations and sizes. A plan for each level shows every pipe, faucet, and drain. Diagrams, details, and schedules also communicate how these components work together to provide a functional plumbing system in a building.

Plumbing plans are usually irrelevant in smaller complexes but increase in importance in larger developments.

Mechanical Sheets: (M Series) The mechanical engineer's drawings will show the locations and sizes of all mechanical equipment in an architectural design. These plans include the size and layout of all exposed or concealed ductwork and the location of each vent, heating unit, cooling unit, and thermostat.

Mechanical plans are usually irrelevant in smaller complexes but increase in importance in larger developments.

Electrical Sheets: (E Series) These drawings will show the locations of all power outlets, sources, light fixtures, and switches. As we see growing trends toward energy efficiency after building occupancy, the electrical drawings may also account for energy and sustainability compliance. Typically, lighting, power and voltage plans are provided for each building level, and a sheet is devoted to power calculations.

Electrical plans are of minor significance in smaller developments but are required in large complexes.

Landscape Architecture Sheets: (L Series) Landscaping plans include natural elements, such as flowers, trees, and grass, as well as manufactured elements, such as parking lots, paths, fountains, and sheds. Landscape designs may also include overlays for irrigation and lighting. The licensed Landscape Architect submits these drawings for the contractors on how to construct the various landscape elements.

This plan provides the basis for most site improvement measurements. If unavailable, the provider must manually measure roads, curbs, sidewalks, and paths and count items like streetlights.

The building plans that providers will use in a Depreciation Report are based on the age and complexity of the development. Based on our experience, the following types of plans are usually required for each property type.

Property Type	G Series	CE Series	A Series	S Series	M Series	E Series	L Series
Bare Land	X	X					X
Bare Land with Clubhouse	X	X	X				X
Townhome	X	X	X				X
Low Rise	X	X	X				X
High-rise	X	X	X	X	X	X	X
Industrial	X	X	X	X			X

If you recall, I stated the first question that councils ask providers is, *"Do I need the plans?"*

My answer was that the truth lies between the age and complexity of the development.

Readers need to understand how a strata plan is created. The strata plan measures the outer perimeter of the strata lots. In a townhome or building, it is 50% of the way through the exterior wall of the building, that being the wood framing or the concrete wall. The interior common hallway is also halfway through the framing for the wall to which the drywall is attached. For this reason, buildings are surveyed for strata plans when they are framed. A wood-framed building does not include exterior siding or interior wall materials. This measurement method means there will be a slight undercount for the wall perimeter length and area if only the strata plan is used.

In a bare land development, the strata plan measures the boundaries of the strata lots and the common property, the sidewalks, roadways, and parks if included. If the water and sanitary services are from the local municipality or regional district, there is usually no problem if the plans are unavailable.

Generally, multifamily developments had basic construction features until the 1985 building code changes. The 1985 revisions allowed many new architectural features and types of siding, like acrylic stucco, which eventually led to the leaky condo crisis in British Columbia. Estimates are that approximately 45% of the 159,979 strata units constructed in B.C. between 1985 and 2000 were found to have envelope leak problems. The 1998 building code changes corrected many of the issues that had allowed this crisis.

Concerning the question of requiring plans for townhomes and low-rise buildings, as the construction was basic, usually, plans are not required for townhomes or low-rise wood frame buildings built before the code change. As the buildings can take two to three years to build, any strata built before 1987 usually do not need drawings. Providers will use the strata plans and measure on-site.

This statement is not an absolute rule.

British Columbia's strata legislation has gone through three major changes. The first legislation was a basic set of laws in 1966 called the Strata Titles Act. In 1974, the Condominium Act came into force. The most recent legislation, the Strata Property Act, was enacted in 1998 and came into force in 2000.

Under Section 006 of the Condominium Act, if approved by the land title office registrar, a strata lot could include balconies, patios, private yard areas, garages, parking spaces, storage areas and other areas and spaces not enclosed by floors, walls, or ceilings.

The Land Title Office Registrar approved these from 1974 to around 1977, allowing several developments to have the decks or balcony included in the strata lot. This approval allowed the strata lot boundaries to exist outside the building envelope. The surveyor did not measure the building perimeter wall on the strata plan, so without confirmation, the strata plan cannot be relied upon. Fortunately, with laser tools and AutoCAD measuring software, this is now a minor inconvenience.

But it does raise a legal issue:

If a strata lot includes a patio or balcony, who is responsible for repairing it?

The balcony is not CP or LCP, since it is inside the strata lot. In most cases, it should be the owner's responsibility.

However, under the Strata Property Regulations regarding Depreciation Reports, such a balcony is outside the building envelope and usually would be the strata's responsibility under the legislation.

I believe these patios and decks are outside the building envelope. Therefore, for the purpose of Depreciation Reports, they are common property, meaning the Strata Corporation is responsible.

But in scenarios where the council disagrees with my opinion, I believe that the Strata Corporation needs a legal opinion that the Depreciation Report provider can rely on.

But back to the plans, and if they are required at all.

We have found that most areas outside the Lower Mainland and Greater Victoria continued basic construction techniques for buildings before 2000. So, in many cases, the strata plan may be the only plan required in these areas. A review with online mapping from Google or local governments will assist the provider in making an educated decision about whether the need for building plans is reasonable.

The 1998 Building Code instituted rain screening and other strategies to lessen the problems that led to the crisis. But it still permitted projections and multiple layered roofs that cannot be measured without drawings. Therefore, to determine if the strata plan is sufficient for a complex where the strata plan is registered after January 1, 2000, the provider normally will do a review on a property-by-property basis.

One hard and fast rule is that building plans are required if there are three or more types of siding, if the walls of each floor on a townhome or apartment building are a different size, or if the roof has more than two elevations.

High-rises always require plans.

Maintenance Documents

Operating Guides - Manuals and guides can provide valuable data about operating equipment, like boilers and hot water tanks. They are usually located in the mechanical rooms in a file or the building office. Having them available during the inspection is usually all that is needed.

Warranty Documents - These documents are provided when purchasing or replacing new assets or components. They provide useful information about these items.

Maintenance History Guide - This is a list of suppliers and costs for past repairs or replacements for major work done around the building. Developments should attempt to keep a list of what was repaired or replaced, the reason for the work, the date, the supplier, the cost, and the location.

Asset Inventory List - Providers need to know the history of asset replacement. Assets, commonly referred to as Furniture, Fixtures, and Equipment (FF&E), are usually not attached to the building. These items are in the lobby, laundry room, gym, pool, kitchen, common areas, and guest suites. This list indicates the location, when the strata purchased it, the cost and the supplier. If this does not exist, it is a good idea to create one for insurance purposes.

Consulting Reports

Specialist Reports for Roofing, Elevators, Plumbing and Electrical issues - Specialists are usually brought in because the complex has a concern or maintenance is required on something that does not require an engineer. Providers cannot take apart some equipment under provincial safety restrictions and regulations. Therefore, specialist reports provide the information necessary to complete a comprehensive analysis.

Electrical Planning Reports - These are one-time reports required by the end of 2026 or 2028, depending on where you live. They discuss the electrical capacity of the development, peak requirements, load availability and projected requirements. Please see Chapter 5 for a more fulsome discussion.

Engineer Reports - Engineers are usually brought in when there are mould or structural issues, a warranty review is required, or a Building Envelope Condition Assessment (BECA) report needs to be prepared.

Prior Depreciation Report - Prior reports can provide helpful information, yet most providers will not provide an updated report based on data from another firm's report. Some reasons include that the former provider did not provide the unit counts or measurements, the measurements appeared incorrect or vague, or the former provider used a different measurement method.

Missing or misleading data can confuse a reader on quantity take-offs, costings, or lifespans, which leads to bunching. Bunching is described in a later chapter.

When a provider agrees to rely on the prior report data, the previous quantities (unit counts or measurements) are assumed to be accurate. However, the inspection will still be required to confirm their existence and condition. If the data is incorrect, the update will become a full report for an additional fee.

Special Situations

Sectioned Building

A sectioned building is a mixed-use building. Each building section must have a different use, usually with separate access. Each section operates separately from other parts of the building.

An example is a 4-storey building with a 3-level residential section over the main level retail section, with a common (joint-use) section. The residential section concerns itself with the limited common property for residential units, while the retail section concerns itself with the limited commercial common property. The joint-use section concerns itself with the common shared property, including the lobby, elevator, roof, balconies, building envelope, windows, doors, and shared parking area.

Within this building, each section has its own operating budget, CRF, and bylaws. Therefore, each section must provide a current copy of its bylaws with three years of CRF contributions, interest income, and year-end financial statements.

The complex should have a Reciprocal Cost Agreement (RCA). These documents discuss the access rights and the financial obligations of all users. Providers separate the section's financial responsibilities based on the allocation of costs as outlined in the RCA. This document may or may not be registered on Title. The RCA may also be in the bylaws or the original disclosure agreements.

It is the complex's responsibility to provide the RCA. If no such document is available, most providers will ask the building management for a legal opinion on the cost allocation.

In sectioned buildings, sometimes each section can have its own property manager. Most providers will not start a complex unless the building strata council and the section councils have all agreed to participate. No provider wants to complete part of a complex.

Is it a Type or a Section?

A complex can have more than one type. A "Type" is a building in a strata plan that is different from another kind of building, like a townhome, as opposed to an apartment building.

Within a strata plan with two or more building types, the annual administration costs can be separated by types, not by the CRF. There is only one reserve account for the complex, and therefore, there is only one Depreciation Report.

If requested, most providers can break down the buildings in the report so that each strata council can look at the issues with each building, but the provider cannot separate the building types into different reports.

The information requirements would be the same as if it were just a single building.

Privacy Rights for Sections

I have seen several reports where the Depreciation Report for each section is combined into one report. This is commonly referred to as a Combined Depreciation Report. This type of report is not permitted, as the financials and the funding choices of one section are shown to people in another section.

The Personal Information Protection Act (PIPA) of British Columbia and the Personal Information and Electronics Documents Act (PIPEDA) set out requirements for how organizations collect, use, disclose, and secure personal information. I have been advised that for privacy reasons, providers cannot disclose the financial details of one section to anyone outside the section without 100% consent of all owners.

A common question is, what if the majority agree to a Combined Depreciation Report?

Unfortunately, the agreement must include 100% of all registered owners, as the majority present at a legally called meeting cannot override the legal privacy rights of those not in attendance. In practical terms, this is not achievable. Therefore, the commercial section cannot see the residential section's report, and vice versa.

However, the legislation implies that the entire building's physical condition assessment must be shown to all owners. In addition, some lawyers have indicated that the other section's physical analysis is not protected under the same privacy legislation.

As such, each owner can expect one report. The physical inspection results of all sections are shown in the report. Still, each section receives the financial data for its area of responsibility and the shared (joint use) common property. The financial details of the other sections are not disclosed.

Shared Amenities

Shared amenities can be as simple as a shared roadway between two or more developments or as complex as a clubhouse and pool shared by four or more neighbouring developments. These amenities are accessed through easements.

Easements give a person who is not an owner the right to access a road or path on the Strata Corporation's property. This right is typically required for a shared roadway or access to an amenity building. Easements are registered on Title and usually state the shared-cost agreement.

These amenities should have a separate operating account and CRF account. If it is a more extensive amenity, it may even have bylaws. All Strata Corporations that pay for a shared amenity have a legal interest and should receive a copy of the Depreciation Report.

Privacy Rights for Shared Amenities

Like sections, due to privacy regulations, providers cannot provide financial information about one development to another, so the preferred solution is a separate report for the shared amenity area alone. This regulation means the provider must legally contract with all the corporations involved. While it may be on one complex's property, all the complexes involved have legal and financial interests.

Sometimes, a participating Strata Corporation is unwilling to enter a contract for a supplementary report covering the shared amenities. This lack of enthusiasm can relate to costs, as there is usually an additional fee. Other times, they may feel it is somebody else's problem, as it is not on their property. However, most of the time, they think the Strata Corporation, with the amenities on their property, will give them the details. These council members must understand that the other council members would be breaching the privacy rights of their owners by disclosing private financial information.

Some providers have tried to resolve this conflict of interest by including only the proportional cost for the shared amenity in the Depreciation Report. However, this can become confusing for report updates or renewals.

There is a question whether the Strata Corporation that did not participate in the supplementary report is in breach of the Strata Property Act, as there is no report on assets for which they are responsible.

Another solution is when one Strata Corporation, usually the one with the largest financial interest, pays for the supplementary report. In this situation, the other complexes must only give authorization. After completing, all parties receive the supplemental report.

Again, the provider requires a current copy of their bylaws (if they have any), the RCA, easements, three years of CRF contributions, interest income, and year-end financial statements.

For minor shared amenities, sometimes there may be a handshake agreement. The provider will need an email from all the strata representatives confirming the cost arrangement. But if no cost agreement is available and nobody can agree, a legal opinion may be the last option.

Air Space Parcel (ASP)

An Air Space Parcel (ASP) is a surveyed three-dimensional air parcel. The ASP can be within another building's envelope, like in a downtown high-rise complex, meaning there can be one or several air space parcels within one building. Alternatively, the ASP can be just outside the building envelope, like in the case of townhomes.

In all cases, there is what appraisers call the remainder parcel, a building that the ASP is in the middle of, or on land owned by another party.

The building maintenance and operation rights and responsibilities are listed within an Air Space Parcel Agreement, a document between 100-300 pages or more. ASP Agreements are registered on Title. These complexes do not need a separate reciprocal cost agreement, as these are covered as part of the ASP document. It is the complex's responsibility to provide these documents.

When evaluating a Strata Corporation that is the remainder site, the ASP agreement from the air parcels is required to determine any cost implications and contributions. The remainder parcel Strata would be treated as any other strata property in other data requests.

When evaluating a Strata Corporation within the ASP portion in a complex, the ASP agreement also needs review for the same reason. Like the remainder site portion of the property, the ASP should provide its own operating budget, financials, and bylaws.

Unlike sections, a joint-use committee may not be applicable.

Privacy Rights for Air Space Parcels (ASP)

Like with sections, privacy regulations do not allow financial information to be provided to another party outside the ASP Strata Corporation. Therefore, only the owners within the ASP will receive the Depreciation Report.

Chapter 13 – Classes of Depreciation Reports

There are three main classes of Depreciation Reports, each with its own level of document requirements. Understanding them will allow the Strata Council or Property Manager to collect the appropriate data, as discussed in the previous chapter.

Classes of Depreciation Reports

1. Comprehensive Depreciation Report
2. Updated Depreciation Report
3. Financial Update
4. Preliminary Depreciation Report

Comprehensive Depreciation Report (Depreciation Report With a Site Visit)

In a Comprehensive Depreciation Report, the expectation is that the provider starts from nothing, meaning there is no relevant data. Therefore, councils must supply the provider with as much information as possible to produce a reliable report.

As previously stated, the older the complex, the less likely the building plans or maintenance documents will be available. The provider will be aware of this issue.

Many Strata Corporations repeatedly complete the equivalent of a "first" Depreciation Report because either the previous firm is out of business, the cost is too high for the renewal, or they did not like the report.

When a provider agrees to rely on the prior report data, the previous quantities (unit counts or measurements) must be accurate. If a provider lacks confidence in the preceding report's quantities, they will not provide a new report based on the other firm's data.

This occurs when the prior report unit counts or measurements are not provided in the report, as was discussed in Chapter 11. Reports that do not state the number of components, like sliding doors, but just a total replacement cost, are hard to rely on.

It could also be that the measurements appear incorrect or vague or were determined using a method different from the new provider's. For example, the report states that the carpeting was installed between 2010 and 2015, not indicating the actual year.

Another example is when doors are measured by square feet (which architects utilize), but this is not how most others in the reserve planning field measure doors.

If a provider agrees to rely on the prior report and adjusts the fee downwards, the inspection will still be required to confirm their existence and condition. If the data is incorrect, the discount will be removed, creating conflict with the Property Manager and Strata Council. The result is that most providers will look at the prior report and use what they can but charge and operate as if it were a Comprehensive Depreciation Report.

Updated Depreciation Report (Depreciation Report Update With a Site Visit)

An Updated Depreciation Report aims to update a current report at the end of the renewal period. The renewal period in British Columbia is now 5 years.

The only difference between a Comprehensive and an Updated Depreciation Report is that no component inventory is completed. In other words, nothing is counted or measured, as all previous measurements are assumed to be correct. The provider expects to have all the data from the Comprehensive Depreciation Report and any intervening Depreciation Reports without a Site Visit.

When the legislation required a report every three years, most providers agreed to perform two to three updates before insisting on a comprehensive report again. Under the 2024 changes that allowed a new report every five years, the industry is moving to one update, so a comprehensive Depreciation Report is completed every ten years.

As an update, the current bylaws, the minutes, AGM/SGM notices, and minutes since the last report are required. In addition, if the provider uses questionnaires, the council should return a summary version focusing on the previous three years.

On the financial side, providers will request the CRF contributions, interest, and the fiscal year-end financial statements since the last report. These are usually attached to the AGM notices.

The council should provide any changes to the alteration agreement summary, the list of leases or licenses for equipment or services, changes to third-party use agreements, or recent lawsuits or arbitration decisions.

New operating guides, warranty documents, an updated maintenance history guide, and asset inventory lists are also required.

Lastly, new specialists' reports for roofing, elevators, plumbing and electrical issues, or recent engineer reports, must be provided.

If you are in a sectioned building, you need the most up-to-date bylaws for each section and any changes to the RCA. Financially, you also need all building sections' CRF contributions, interest, and fiscal year-end financial statements.

If you are in a building with ASPs, the most current bylaws are necessary. Financially, the CRF contributions, interest, and fiscal year-end financial statements for all ASP portions in the building are required.

If you share amenities with another corporation, the most current bylaws and any change to the RCA need to be reviewed. The CRF contributions, interest, and fiscal year-end financial statements are also required.

Financial Update to the Depreciation Report (Depreciation Report without a Site Visit)

A Financial Update to the Depreciation Report, or a Depreciation Report without a site visit, is only used to update the existing funding plans. No inspection is required. As such, it does not count as a Depreciation Report under the *Strata Property Act*.

The provider expects to have all the data from the last Comprehensive or Updated Depreciation Report. This report updates the funding plan to consider current contributions, special levies, price changes, inflation, and interest rates. There is an assumption that everything has stayed the same regarding the physical condition of the building. Given this, the data requirements are limited.

The only documents required for this report are financial, which include the CRF contributions, interest, and fiscal year-end financial statements since the last report.

All sections, ASP Strata Corporations, joint-use committees, and shared amenities must provide the most recent financial documents.

For large properties (more than 200 units), there is a consensus that owners should conduct this type of report annually to update the existing report's financial projections.

Developments that were in poor financial shape initially but have substantially increased their contributions may want to get a financial update to boost the confidence of owners and potential buyers. In addition, insurers or lenders may want a report if they are concerned about a client's fiscal health.

These reports are inappropriate if there has been a significant renovation or repair. These changes require resetting the lifespan of the items replaced, which involves reinspection. A comprehensive report is usually needed in this situation.

Preliminary Depreciation Report (Not Yet Constructed)

Preliminary Depreciation Reports are prepared before or during construction and are used for budget estimates. They are based on design documents, such as architectural and engineering plans.

The Depreciation Report provider completes a component inventory based on the building plans, determines the lifespan and related cost estimates, and recommends a funding plan. No condition assessment is completed, nor is an analysis of the reserve fund status possible. This type of report aims to determine the CRF contributions during occupancy.

As of May 2024, no province in Canada, including British Columbia, requires preliminary reports.

A chart on the following page indicates the document requirements for each of the main classes of Depreciation Reports.

Physical Analysis Review Checklist - Data Collection				
Data Collection: Required		First Report	Updated Report	Financial Update
1	Strata Plans		▓	▓
2	Current Bylaws			▓
3	Alteration Agreements Summary			▓
4	Lawsuits or Arbitration Decisions			▓
5	Leases or Licenses for Equipment or Services			▓
6	Third Party Use Agreements			▓
7	Provider's Questionnaire			
8	Minutes, AGM/SGM Notices, and Results			
9	Three Years of CRF Contributions, Interest as well as Fiscal Year-End Financial Statements.			▓
10	Last Year of CRF Contributions, Interest as well as Fiscal Year-End Financial Statements.	▓	▓	
Data Collection: If You Have Them				
1	Architectural (A Series)		▓	▓
2	Mechanical (M Series)		▓	▓
3	Electrical (E Series)		▓	▓
4	Site (S Series)		▓	▓
5	Landscaping (L Series)		▓	▓
6	Operating Guides			▓
7	Warranty Documents			▓
8	Maintenance History Guide			▓
9	Asset Inventory List			▓
10	Specialists Reports for Roofing, Elevators, Plumbing and Electrical issues			▓
11	Engineer Reports			▓
12	Prior Depreciation Reports		▓	▓

		Data Collection: Sectioned Buildings - Required			
	1	All Current Section Bylaws			
	2	Reciprocal Cost Agreements			
	3	Easements			
	4	Three Years of CRF Contributions, Interest as well as Fiscal Year-End Financial Statements, for all sections in a building.			
	5	Last Year of CRF Contributions, Interest as well as Fiscal Year-End Financial Statements.			
		Data Collection: Shared Amenities - If You Have Them			
	1	Current Bylaws for the shared amenity			
	2	Reciprocal Cost Agreement			
	3	Easements			
	4	Three Years of CRF Contributions, Interest as well as Fiscal Year-End Financial Statements, for the shared amenity.			
	5	Last Year of CRF Contributions, Interest as well as Fiscal Year-End Financial Statements.			
		Data Collection: Air Parcel Agreements - Required			
	1	Current Bylaws			
	2	Air Space Parcel (ASP) Agreements			
	3	Easements			
	4	Three Years of CRF Contributions, Interest as well as Fiscal Year-End Financial Statements.			
	5	Last Year of CRF Contributions, Interest as well as Fiscal Year-End Financial Statements.			

Chapter 14 – Selection of the Components

This chapter discusses the selection guidelines in more detail regarding what should be funded through the CRF and, therefore, be included in the Depreciation Report. This flowchart indicates the process to determine if the components under review should be in the Depreciation Report.

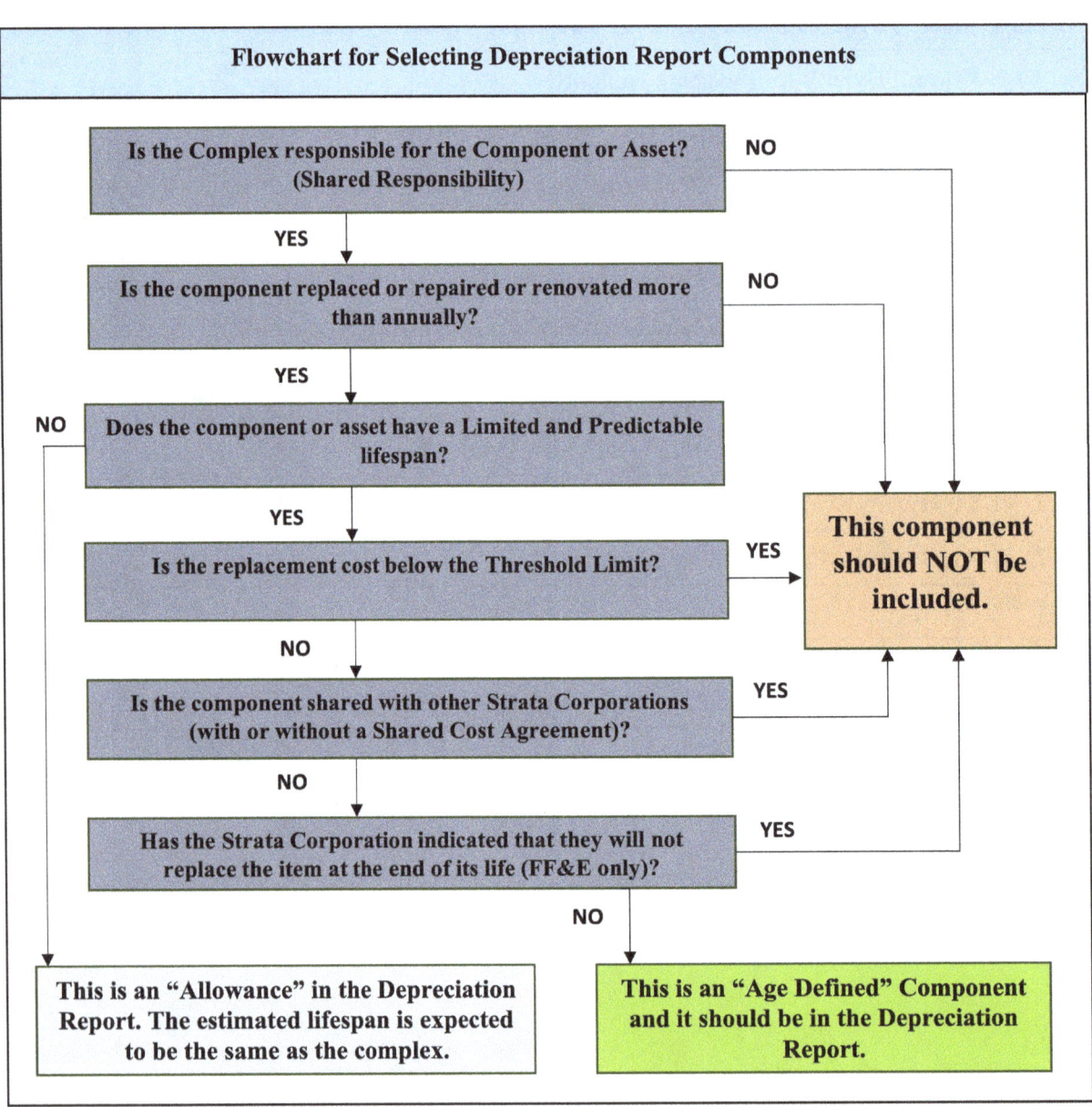

After collecting the documents, the provider must understand what to include in the component inventory.

STEP 1: Common Responsibility

The underlying principle for providers is that only components and assets that are shared responsibility are in the report.

Condominiums have been sold as carefree living, yet they are based on paying others to maintain the shared buildings and assets. Common area responsibilities are set out in the *Strata Property Act* and Regulations.

Within a residential or commercial building, legislation states that shared or common responsibilities include the following:

1. Structural and architectural components, including the foundations, exterior doors, exterior wall siding and wall features, windows, entry and sliding doors, parking doors, decks, balconies, railings, carports, and painting.
2. Roofing components include roofing material, skylights, drainage, soffits, and fascia.
3. Interior components, including flooring, painting or other wall treatments, interior doors, and windows.
4. Conveyancing components, including the elevator and wheelchair lift systems.
5. Electrical components, including the distribution system in the building, the interior lights and fire panel, the building security and access system, exterior lights, and fixtures on or around the exterior of the building.
6. Mechanical System components, including the complex's water and sanitary drainage systems, fire systems, hot water systems, HVAC systems, and septic fields.
7. Amenity components include the clubhouse building envelope and roof, the interior finishing, furniture, fixtures, and equipment of the amenity areas, including common rooms, guest suites, and recreation areas, including the pool/saunas or hot tub.
8. Site components, including the grounds, paths and patios, interior roadways, water features, outdoor recreation, fencing, site security, complex signage, and freestanding service buildings.

For bare land complexes, legislation states common responsibilities include the following:

1. Electrical components, including the distribution system to the lots, as well as exterior lights and fixtures not on lots:
2. Mechanical system components include the complex's water and sanitary drainage systems, fire systems, and septic fields.

3. Amenity components include the clubhouse building envelope and roof, the interior finishing, furniture, fixtures, and equipment of the amenity areas, including common rooms, guest suites, and recreation areas, including pools/saunas or hot tubs.
4. Site components, including the grounds, paths and patios, interior roadways, water features, outdoor recreation, fencing, site security, complex signage, and freestanding service buildings.

The rule of thumb is that all building components and assets not in a strata lot are Common Property (CP) or Limited Common Property (LCP); therefore, they are common responsibility.

Even if a component is within a strata lot, items can be deemed common property within a building. An example is a water distribution pipe in a wall between units. As discussed earlier, this is legislated as part of the common responsibility.

LCP is common property that is for the exclusive use of one or more units. Patios, balconies, or terraces accessible by occupants in one or two units are typical examples. Another common LCP allocation is parking stalls that are for the use of one unit. Elevators can be restricted to a single or a few users in higher-end buildings. Many townhome complexes have rear yards with fencing, attached garage interior space, or detached carports that are LCP areas, even though the owners operate as though it's their personal space.

Under the *Strata Property Act*, LCP must be kept clean by the strata lots with access. Still, all maintenance and repair work is the Strata Corporation's responsibility according to the Standard Bylaws.

Occasionally, the bylaws state that some items on or attached to the common property are the owners' responsibility. These items usually relate to LCP improvements, developer installations, or openings. Openings are anything that penetrates the exterior roof or envelope of the building, including doors, windows, sliding doors, skylights, vents, plugs, and gas and water hook-up bibs. The goal of using bylaws to shift costs to owners is to make the development look financially stronger or to assist owners who do not have the money to pay the special levy for the required work.

Courts historically have interpreted openings and developer installations as being shared responsibility. Although bylaws are registered, this does not mean they are legal; it only means they are registered. A tribunal or court confirms the legality of the bylaws only after a complaint is made about them.

Given this information, most providers will not produce reports that pass on these shared costs to owners. Besides being on the side of case law and the intent of the legislation, standards-based report providers use this methodology as it provides consistency and transparency.

Items attached to common property, like satellite dishes, new skylights, or sunshades, should only be allowed with alteration agreements. As the item attached will usually cause the component to fail faster, meaning a convenience permitted to one owner may have a substantial cost to everyone later. However, the responsibility lies with the owner who installed it.

Of course, a Strata Corporation sometimes takes responsibility for these issues unexpectedly. An example is when an opening, such as a skylight, was permitted to be installed after construction without an alteration agreement. The verbal agreement is disputed years later when maintenance is required, which can be years after new owners have moved in. The written agreement can easily get lost, and because of the time and cost to litigate the issue, the skylight usually becomes grandfathered, with the Strata Corporation assuming responsibility.

Developer-installed components on or attached to common property can never be charged to the owners. An example is a carport in front of each unit; the unit resident is the only person using it. Another typical example is fencing installed by the developer. Even if the owner replaced them later, they are always the Strata Corporations' responsibility, and bylaws cannot shift costs to owners.

However, there are some exceptions.

The first exception is self-administered damage. I refer to it as the "baseball rule." Unless you can identify the perpetrator, the complex pays if a baseball goes through a window from the outside. The owner pays if the damage (baseball) comes from the inside.

The second exception is when the owners never owned the asset. This exception occurs when the common area is being leased out, and the tenant owns the items in the common area. Another example is when the owners lease an asset, like laundry machines.

The final exception is a legal decision of a tribunal or court. These are always specific to the development. These decisions must be noted in the report and followed.

One increasing trend we have noticed is a failure to expense components fully. This flaw occurs when the provider fails to account for work fully and only accounts for a portion of the work, leading to partially funded contributions.

These are identifiable in the building components description section by comments such as:

> *"A budget equal to 75% of the estimated cost of the component is provided for periodic major repairs every 20 years."*

The legality of the statement is suspect as the legislation requires a complete replacement in the Depreciation Report, not a partial replacement.

The financial modelling is also not reasonable. You will fall short if you only budget $75,000 to replace something that costs $100,000 before inflation. The only choice is to defer it, which will cost more later, or need a special levy of at least $25,000.

This partial cost estimate is designed to lower the expenses and, thus, the required monthly CRF contributions. However, a group of partially funded components will lead to unsupportable budgeting assumptions, causing "unforeseen" expenses and owner hardship to the point of possible foreclosures.

Sections

As described earlier, some buildings are set up with owners with different uses and access, thus managing themselves as sections. The fact a building has sections is immaterial in the component selection process.

Phases

Phases are portions of a site built and registered at different times. For example, a 5-phase plan may have a situation where a developer built one group of homes, sold it out and then went on to the next phase or group of houses. It may have been over a couple of years or as long as 20 years. Phased developments are covered in the same report; however, the provider should separate components costing based on how years apart the buildings were constructed. One rule of thumb is three years, meaning the same component from several phases is listed in the inventory together if constructed within a three-year timespan. The same component is listed twice if the phases are more than three years apart. However, the fact that a strata development was built over several years is immaterial in the component selection process.

STEP 2: Is the component replaced, repaired, or renovated more than annually?

No matter how large the expenditure, expenses that occur within 12 months are excluded from the CRF budget. These expenses are reasonably predictable in terms of both frequency and cost. They are dealt with in the annual operating budget. Only components and assets that the council cannot budget annually are in the component inventory.

STEP 3: Limited and Predictable Lifespan

Only expenses with a predictable lifespan should be selected. Predicting unreliable income, such as transfers from annual operating budgets or unpredictable costs, such as fire, flood, or earthquake damage, is inappropriate.

All components are separated into two categories called *"age-defined"* or *"allowances."* Components that last the life of the complex are called *"allowances"* and will be discussed in a later section of the book.

"Age defined" expenses have a limited lifespan, meaning they will need to be replaced at least once during the lifespan of the development. Their lifespans are predictable, meaning how long they will last is generally accepted. An example of an "age-defined" expense is exterior painting. In the Lower Mainland, it is customary to repaint the exterior of a wood frame building every ten years. Therefore, one should expect a painting expense in the report every ten years.

Some age-defined components are longer term, like vinyl siding, which has a 50-year life. If the strata ordered the Depreciation Report in the 10th year since installation and the siding was in average shape, readers would expect the remaining life to be 40 years.

Some providers have interpreted this as meaning if the replacement year is outside the 30-year legislated projection period, the provider could drop it from the component list. This practice is unacceptable, as the legislation does not discuss allowing exceptions. In addition, this is a fundamental error that will damage the report from that point on. This error can be expensive because it is usually a big-ticket item, such as a roof replacement.

All financial models are designed to save an equal amount (replacement cost/remaining lifespan in years) annually. So, in the vinyl siding example, if the siding costs $500,000 after 50 years, the development would have to save $10,000 annually, even if the expense is too far away to be in the projection period. If the provider only showed this expense during the last 30 years, the complex would have to save $16,667 annually and lose ten years of tax-free interest income.

Financially, this methodology benefits the current users; however, when the expense suddenly appears ten years later in a report as a line item, it may cause hardships. Again, the legality may be an issue, as the Strata Property Act does not state that expenditures can be disregarded if outside the 30-year projection period.

STEP 4: The Minimum Threshold Limit

The strata legislation does not discuss a minimum dollar value limit for components, though every Depreciation Report contract has one. The threshold limit clause states that providers will not add anything under a certain minimum level (say $1,000) into the Depreciation Report, as the annual operating budget within the repair and maintenance category will most likely handle it. This rule represents the reality of all developments. The threshold limit will be listed in the contract proposal.

Items below the threshold limit are not included in the component inventory, but this does not mean providers should disregard them. In all cases, disclosure is required so the reader knows of any exclusions.

There are two ways that this minimum threshold rule can create reports that are not credible.

The first problem is when the minimum threshold amount is too high. This action reduces the money required in the CRF. These excluded items will take a significant part of the annual operating budget for repairs and maintenance if work is needed.

I have seen a $5,000 threshold level in a report for a small complex. It defies the credibility that the owners would allow a $5,000 expense without discussion at the AGM. In contrast, a Strata Corporation with a concrete high-rise tower, a large mixed-use podium, and a significant amenities center may let this pass.

The upper limit of the threshold clause should be based on a percentage of the operating budget. My firm uses 1% of the operating budget. This method determines the threshold level by the size of the complex.

The second problem occurs when the threshold allowance is applied on a per-unit basis rather than for the entire category. The governing rule is that the threshold limit applies to the total value of all the components in a category, not each component.

For example, an exterior electrical plug on a deck or patio may cost $150 per unit. If the threshold exclusion limit is $1,000 in a six-plex, the total cost would be $900. This total would fall below the threshold limit and be excluded from the report.

In an 80-unit building, the same category total would be $12,000, well above any reasonable lower exclusion limit, and should be included in the report.

In both cases, the misapplication will damage the report's usefulness, underfund the complex, and create unexpected special levies in later reports. These types of errors are usually accompanied by a lack of disclosure of what is being removed under the threshold clause. These errors can make readers lose confidence in the report, as they become aware that many small but noticeable components have been left out.

STEP 5: Are there Shared Amenities?

Shared amenities are usually on one Strata Corporation's property, with shared access and use rights for other Strata Corporations in exchange for shared management and costs.

Shared amenities are treated similarly to sections of a Strata Corporation with privacy rights for all Strata Corporations. Distribution of the Strata Corporation Depreciation Report where the amenity is located to those outside the development is prohibited under privacy legislation, as discussed in the last chapter. It needs a separate Depreciation Report, usually in summary format.

As the amenity area components are included in the supplementary report, they are excluded from the Depreciation Report of the Strata Corporation, where they are located.

STEP 6: Decommissioning Assets at the End of Its Life (FF&E Only)

The Strata Council can make decisions regarding an asset, specifically when to replace a piece of equipment, such as a pool table. The general rule is that the Strata Corporation must replace all assets at the end of their lifespan. Therefore, creating a report with the decommissioning or removal of an asset is more complex.

Strata legislation enables council members to make decisions for the current year but does not allow them to bind future councils. However, they usually have the political pulse of the complex and represent the current owner's intent concerning how the asset replacement will occur. So, if the strata representative states that the owners will not replace the pool table, that is usually their plan.

Suppose the council requests the removal of the asset, such as the pool table. In that case, a hypothetical condition must appear in the report. Standards-based providers will list the applicable asset within the report, clearly identifying to any reader that the provider removed it from the component inventory with an explanation and a statement disclosing that a future council may request it to be reinstated. After all, 15 years later, the driving force of a council may be to replace the pool table, something the earlier council may have had no interest in replacing. The error occurred not when the provider removed it but in not revealing that they removed it from the Depreciation Report.

At the time of the next Depreciation Report inspection, the provider would confirm the removal with the current council representative or put the asset back into the report.

Sometimes, there are larger items to consider, such as playgrounds or excess parking. Providers are not expected to review a complex's zoning and development permit. Still, they need to understand that the developer most likely installed features such as these in exchange for allowing the development to be constructed. The Strata Council cannot remove these items without municipal permission; therefore, the provider cannot remove them from a report.

As a side note, when the council allows an owner to leave "donated items" behind, like gym equipment or furniture, these items become part of the inventory of shared assets and must be included in future reports.

Is This an Allowance?

As mentioned, components that last the life of the structure are called *"allowances."* These components are not expected to be replaced during the life of the building. There is a more expansive definition in the appendix.

While replacement is not predictable, it is prudent to make an allowance available for the deterioration of components, such as underground concrete foundations and most types of servicing. The Strata Corporation should set an amount aside based on the possibility that lifetime components may unexpectedly need repair during the lifespan of the complex.

Allowances are handled in two ways:

The first method lists each allowance component in the building as a line item. A nominal amount or portion of the total replacement cost is allocated as an allowance. This amount is a percentage of the total cost based on the risk of failure. This system allows the complex's aggregate (total) allowances to be utilized if a single allowance-type component fails.

It also allows the allowances to be adjusted downward towards the end of the life of the building if the Strata Council takes that decision. This methodology is preferred by most providers, as there is full disclosure.

The second method does not list individual components on the Benchmark Analysis spreadsheet. Here, an allowance percentage is listed at the bottom of the component inventory as a fixed amount, for instance, 10%. To be transparent, a notation of which components this percentage refers to is required. This methodology often lacks full disclosure and can create errors in mathematical modelling if not done correctly.

The defining characteristic of allowances is that no expenditure for this item is indicated during the projected cash-flow period despite the age of the complex.

Some providers are inserting the term "allowances" into age-defined types of expenses, such as painting. Painting is a regular and predictable event. This method is a poor understanding of terminology, and providers who use such terminology should be avoided.

Other providers feel that if a component does not fail during the lifespan of the development, it need not be accounted for in the report. In such cases, it is intentionally excluded.

Proponents of this philosophy do not believe in allowances. They think that as it is not predictable, they should not include it. Yet, life is full of items that fail when they should not, such as cracking concrete. When something like this fails, it is expensive to correct.

Financially, if you do not have allowances in a report, or if one of these items fails or needs repair, it will be a financial earthquake to the CRF and may lead to a foreclosure risk within the development.

If the components have the characteristics in this chapter's flowchart and the above descriptions, they will be included in the report.

Chapter 15 - Separation of the Components

Once selected, components are tested to determine if they should be identified together or separated in a Depreciation Report. This separation is required for the financial modelling to work correctly. The keys for the 3-part test are use, cost and lifespan.

This flowchart provides a path to determine when a component can be included in a category or must be a separate line item in the report. The first step is determining the use.

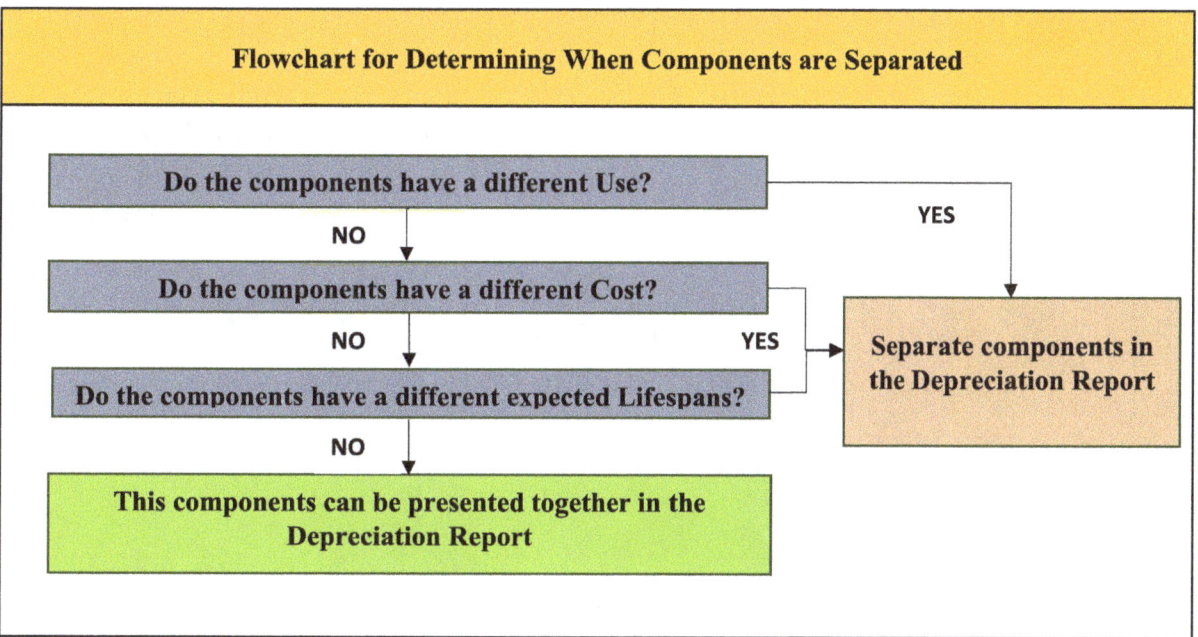

Components with different uses, like exterior siding and roofing materials, should be separated in the report. Items with similar uses, like doors, need further analysis.

If the use is similar, the second step is to review the cost. If the cost difference is significant, this will trigger a separate component. In our doors example, if the costs for metal service and wood service doors were similar, this would not trigger separation into two groups.

The expected lifespan is the final key determinant. The replacement year will differ when the lifespan differs, meaning the expense is in a different year. Thus, the components are separated into various categories on a report.

Again, using the doors example, if a wood door and a metal door cost the same, they still would be separated as the wood door has a significantly shorter life than the metal door.

One of the most common errors is "bunching" or "grouping." This problem occurs when similar components with different characteristics are listed together in the same line.

One of the most common "bunching" categories is doors. In this example, a provider may put garage doors (25 years), metal service doors (35 years), and suite doors (40 years) in the same category - doors. The lifespans and costs are then averaged out. This results in the projected replacement occurring in the wrong year, with incorrect pricing and incorrect amounts of components to replace or renew. This error makes the report useless for its purpose of financial planning.

Another issue is averaging or blending. It differs from bunching in that the components are properly separated, but then, due to periodic repairs or replacements over several years, the age is averaged. Averaging is acceptable in minor items like lighting, as the effect will be minor.

However, with major items such as siding, this type of component needs to be separated. Failure to properly separate work done in differing years will lead to averaging the cost over the lifespans, meaning costs will appear before or after when needed. Averaging major items usually will leave you short of necessary funds, impacting the reserve adequacy ratio, the Strata Corporation's financial health measurement tool.

Chapter 16 – What to Expect at the Inspection

Completing the Depreciation Report inspection depends on the firm, but there are some basic steps.

First, there is the data-gathering stage. As discussed earlier, the information collected depends on the type of development. The data required for a bare land complex differs vastly from that of a mixed-use residential apartment over a retail unit development. Once the data is in the hands of the provider, the inspection staff puts together a list of components they envision will be on the site. Then, they arrange to inspect the property.

The inspection process is the most important interaction with your provider. It is the most crucial step for the provider in putting together a report.

Typically, one to two days before the inspection, the provider should email or call the person who has been made responsible for showing the inspection team around and confirm that they are ready.

The pre-inspection check-in is how providers determine if there is an inspection problem. Examples of inspection problems that can occur include when the building representative is suddenly unavailable, the service room keys are unavailable, or access to balconies or terraces has not been confirmed.

Most inspectors like to start around 10 a.m. for several reasons. In the summer, people want to do inspections before the day gets too hot, while in the winter, people like to do inspections before the ground gets too slushy. Inspection staff will usually try to get to the development before the appointment to walk around, familiarize themselves with the property, and start taking photos.

Before the provider arrives, they will already have a good idea of the complex's components, like windows and exterior lights. However, they may not know the actual unit count (i.e., the number of windows or exterior lights) or their condition. This preliminary site review can be done before the inspection, especially on a bare land or a smaller development.

Second, most complex representatives are available in the morning after their children go to school or daycare or after they wake up on their day off.

Third, inspecting earlier lessens the impact on the owners' amenities. This courteous gesture is especially valued in a complex with a larger footprint and several outdoor amenities. Facilities like outdoor pools, walking areas, or tennis courts are usually not used until later in the day.

Inspection staff like to work without too much interaction with the development residents. When residents use amenities while providers are trying to inspect them, there are always a lot of similar questions. There can also be delays with people using gender-specific rooms, like washrooms or showers. This limits access and slows down the inspection process.

The inspection process in a bare land complex is fast, typically involving roadways, streetlights, curbs, gutters, fencing, and underground servicing.

In smaller townhome developments without a clubhouse, the inspection is typically the exterior building envelope, roofing, decks, balconies, service closets, security, and site improvements like paths, roadways, lighting, and landscaping.

As we get into larger townhome complexes, there are usually many roadways, streetlights, fire hydrants, landscaping, fencing, playgrounds, gazebos, and benches. Although we would like to measure them before we start walking around with the representative, we have found that this is typically not possible because, in many cases, owners have put up fencing that does not allow access around the complex. This measurement plan means that we require the assistance of a complex representative.

Apartment buildings are either handled bottom-up or top-down, depending on the provider. The inspection will usually start on the roof, going to the lowest part of the complex or starting in the basement and working up to the roof. This inspection system is done so that nothing in the building is missed.

Our firm has found that going top-down is easier for the representative and us. In a low-rise, we will typically walk from the roof through the fire escape on one side of the building, walk down the hallway, then go down a floor on the fire stairwell on the other side of the building before walking the hallway on the next level down. This system is how inspectors pick up things like storage rooms on the upper levels, guest rooms, different ceiling heights, and other components that the provider could not pick up from a strata plan.

High-rises typically have amenities on the top or the bottom few floors for those with residential penthouses. High-rises are similar on most floors. Because of this, there is usually an in-depth inspection of the top few floors, with a sampling of other floors as the inspector goes down, finishing with a more detailed inspection of the lower levels, including the lobby.

Providers are not expected to account for anything within the units; however, this does not mean that providers do not have to go through any units.

Suites with a balcony or a terrace will need to be inspected. Because these are outside the building envelope, the balcony or terrace covering, drainage, and sometimes structure will need to be checked for its condition. It is also the best location for reviewing electrical connections, hinged or sliding balcony doors, sealants around windows, soffits, patio dividers, balcony lighting, and trim around the windows.

At a minimum, at least one balcony on each side of the building and at least one rooftop terrace need to be inspected. The building representative needs to be able to find units with owners in them or have the keys for access. Most inspectors respect the time and will interrupt an inspection plan to go to a suite if the occupant must leave.

Sometimes, the strata representative does not have all the service room keys. This situation creates a significant problem because providers need full access to these areas to photograph and review the equipment. Entry must be available, or the inspector may have to come back when access is open, slowing down the report. Still, more importantly for the client, this second visit is subject to an additional charge.

Interior or exterior amenity spaces are just open spaces on the strata plan. Clubhouses usually just show up as an outline on the plan. However, without building drawings, amenity rooms and clubhouses are inspection-time heavy as there is little data about them before the inspection. However, the report must contain all information about the components and their assets.

The provider must create a floor plan inside the amenity space in an apartment complex or a clubhouse. The provider must then describe the flooring, walls, and ceiling and the condition analyzed. Typically, these spaces will have multiple rooms and doors, kitchen cabinets and counters, appliances, bathroom fixtures, separate hot water tanks, an independent electric panel, a fireplace, and attached lighting, including emergency exit signage. These are usually counted and analyzed on the spot.

Let us not forget the FF&E (Furniture, Fixtures, and Equipment) owned by the Strata Corporation. These items are not attached to the building, like the lobby and amenity room sofas and chairs, tables, TVs, floor lamps, gym equipment, window coverings, pool table, books in the bookcase, landscaping and security equipment, and pots and pans in the amenity room or clubhouse kitchen.

The rule of thumb is that if anything is in an amenity space, whether obtained by purchase or donation, it is an asset of the development and must be replaced at the end of its lifespan. So, if you do not want a piece of furniture in the report, dispose of it before the inspection.

Depending on the complex, this amenity space review takes 15 to 90 minutes. But of course, if the complex has extensive recreational facilities, it could take hours or even days. One inspection of a 300+ unit summer-oriented RV complex on over 50 acres with a beach, two clubhouses, three pools, several changing and shared laundry buildings, a waterpark, a maintenance building, several fields, vehicles, many tennis and pickleball courts, wastewater treatment center, and water treatment centre, took two inspectors two days for the complex's first Depreciation Report.

During inspections, expect the provider to use the amenity space as their office. Most providers will ask that the room be set aside for at least two to three hours during the inspection period. This temporary office will allow the inspection staff to store measuring equipment, make notes, measure, count, and photograph the space efficiently.

The amenity space also allows the provider to ask questions of the council representative without owners walking in every few minutes. After this, providers should be able to complete the inspection and finish in the amenity space without any more assistance.

Sometimes, the information on the council's survey differs from that collected at the inspection. Other times, new data is collected. This can result in more detailed information being required from the strata representative at the end of the inspection. Most firms now send a reminder the day after the inspection to keep everything fresh in their memory.

After the inspection process, the provider will have all the information they need to complete the component inventory, as discussed at the beginning of this section.

Section Three

Financial Analysis

Chapter 17 - Funding Principles

Once the component inventory is complete, the provider can start the financial analysis. Understanding the funding principles, funding choices, and key financial variables will lead to a standards-based Depreciation Report with understandable financial modelling and realistic funding plans.

According to the National Reserve Study Standards from the Community Associations Institute (CAI), the four funding principles balance a funding plan.

Funding Principles

1. Sufficient Cash
2. Stable Contribution Rate
3. Evenly Distributed
4. Fiscally Responsible

The first principle is to design a funding plan to provide the Strata Corporation with enough cash reserves to perform their reserve fund projects when required.

This principle means any funding plan must include contributions, special levies, interest income, and loan proceeds. These are the only four permitted sources of Strata Corporation income in a Depreciation Report.

Many Strata Corporations budget for a surplus annually and deposit the excess into the CRF. This type of income is not steady or predictable and, therefore, cannot be relied upon. Insurance or other legal proceeds are also not a stable source of revenue and cannot be used as revenue. As such, these are not recognized sources for ongoing financial planning.

The second principle is that the development should have a stable contribution rate. Stable refers to a contribution rate that does not change year over year. This is required for proper financial modelling. Chapter 19 discusses this concept in more detail.

When the monthly CRF fee contribution rate is variable, it upsets the third principle: that providers should distribute all contributions evenly.

Theoretically, when a Strata Corporation has a deficiency or insufficient funds in the CRF, it results from the past owners deciding to take the money that was supposed to be in the CRF and invest it into something else or spend it. Truthfully, in most cases, the Strata Corporation was unaware of the required level of contributions.

The reality is that no Strata Corporation in British Columbia is fully funded. As such, the contributions alone will rarely meet the expenditure requirements. That means that when people buy a strata lot, they buy into that deficiency. Owners can reduce this deficiency with increased contributions, periodic special levies, or loans.

Finally, the funding plan must be fiscally responsible. This means a financial strategy that will not cause financial hardship to most owners or impact the market value. We cannot say all owners, as sometimes fixed or low-income owners cannot meet the financial obligations of the complex. While tragic, the decision-makers have a duty to the other owners not to let it fall into disrepair.

Another part of being financially responsible is that the funding plan must be safe for the council members to present to the owners without it being removed at the next AGM.

These principles are the guidelines around the funding plan choices. They are fundamental to proper financial modelling and the analysis of the financial health of Strata Corporations.

Chapter 18 – Funding Choices

We always discuss funding plans and models in Depreciation Report planning. Before discussing models, understanding the types of funding choices in a funding plan is essential.

Funding Choices

1. Contributions
2. Special Levies
3. Strata Loans
4. Deferral

Readers need to understand an underlying concept when making funding choice decisions in a funding plan. While expenses occur periodically over the 30-year projection period, the year that the expenses will occur will never change. This means the only variable in alternate funding models is how the expenses are funded.

The place to start in any funding plan is with the funding status or how much money the Strata Corporation has at the beginning of the report's projection period. Then, the decision-makers can select an appropriate funding plan or decide how the Strata Corporation will raise funds for the future.

When a major repair or replacement is required, a Strata Corporation has four options available to address the expenditure.

The first and most logical way to maintain assets is to have enough money as part of the owner's regular monthly contributions (strata fees) to the CRF.

The second option is to pass a special levy (special assessment) to the ownership in an amount required to cover the expenditure. Special levies can go into the general CRF account or a separate CRF account, such as a roof replacement account. When a special levy is passed, the Strata Corporation has the authority and responsibility to collect the special levies, even through foreclosure, if necessary.

However, a Strata Corporation considering a special levy cannot guarantee that a levy, when needed, will be passed. It has been proven that owners will vote down special assessments for repairs, even when critical. Consequently, the Strata Corporation cannot guarantee its ability to perform the required repairs or replace those major components when needed.

Continual failure to get support for special assessments has led to the appointment of an administrator as council members resign or when owners worried about their equity apply for court intervention. While administrators are rare, their appointment is usually related to underfunding. Once an administrator is appointed, the owners lose any ability to influence funding choices. Strata Corporations are better served to ensure it does not get to this point.

The third option is for the Strata Corporation to borrow money from a lending institution to cover the required repairs. In many cases, banks or third-party providers will lend to a Strata Corporation using "future homeowner contributions" as collateral and the payment source for the loan.

Strata loans are not the best option in most cases. With this method, the current owners are pledging the future assets of a Strata Corporation. They will also incur additional interest and fees on the original principal amount. Other concerns are loan monitoring costs or loss of control of monthly payments, as the lender may have additional requirements to add security to the loan.

The fourth option, too often used, is simply deferral. This choice simply increases the list of maintenance items. The result is an escalation of costs beyond replacement costs. The Strata Corporation's financial ability to catch up is usually low, leading to higher special levies when deferral is no longer possible.

Deferred maintenance can usually be identified as a lack of a current Depreciation Report. It has been common in the past for decision-makers to want to correct deferred maintenance in the complex before ordering the report. However, with the new legislation, this will not be possible. The mandatory requirement for a Depreciation Report will show all the deferred maintenance items.

As interest income depends on contributions and special levies, owners do not directly control it. Therefore, while it is considered income in the prior chapter, it is not deemed a funding choice.

In conclusion, these four options represent the only choices in a funding plan.

Chapter 19 – The Financial Variables

The conversion of physical analysis information into financial information requires three key financial variables. They are the Construction Inflation Rate (CIR), the Investment Interest Rate (IIR) and the Contribution Rate (CR). There are also some important renewal assumptions. Any misapplication of this data will make the report's core purpose – financial planning – unreliable.

> **Financial Variables**
>
> 1. Construction Inflation Rate (CIR)
> 2. Investment Interest Rate (IIR)
> 3. Contribution Rate (CR)
> 4. Renewal Assumptions

The following financial analysis is required by legislation:

1. An inflation rate for major repair or replacement of the common elements and assets of the Strata Corporation at the estimated time of the repair or replacement. This is the Construction Inflation Rate (CIR).

2. The estimated interest rate that the cash and investments in the CRF will earn. This is the Investment Interest Rate (IIR).

Both assist in determining the Contribution Rate (CR), the annual increase rate in owners' annual contributions, excluding special levies. When discussing the funding principles, we stated that the CR had to be stable for the projection period. The CR is expressed as a percentage.

Once the CIR and the IIR have been determined, the provider can establish the Optimal Contribution Rate (OCR). The OCR is the contribution rate that will allow the least impact on the development while ensuring the Strata Corporation increases its financial strength. Reserve adequacy, the internationally accepted method of measuring the financial strength of a Strata, is discussed in Chapter 21 in more detail.

This chapter will discuss these financial variables, how to calculate them, their interrelationship, and the common errors we see.

Construction Inflation Rate (CIR)

The first variable is the CIR. Based on construction cost projections, providers must inflate all future costs for repairing and renovating building components. The CIR should be determined by averaging local construction inflation rates over a longer term, say five to ten years, so sudden economic changes are not utilized for longer-term projections.

This projected inflation rate should be based on defensible third-party research, such as cost manuals or statistics. All reports need a note explaining how the CIR is calculated.

To be fiscally responsible and included in financial models, all funding plans must have a stable construction inflation rate, meaning it does not change over the projection period. If the market conditions change, the following report in five years will reflect a new CIR.

This concept should not be confused with the annual inflation rate (AIR), the annual increase in construction costs used in insurance appraisal reports. It is a short-term rate and reflects the sudden change in pricing (due to shortage or lack of demand) that may not be replicated over several years.

Common Inflation Rate Errors and Consequences

Over or under-estimating the CIR

Underestimating the CIR will result in underestimating expenditures, as the inflation factor is too low. In the short term, there is no real effect. Over the long term, the special levies projected will be too low. This may create a real hardship for owners unprepared for the actual special levies, which may be much larger than they needed to be.

This will also make any financial modelling in the short term and the longer term irrelevant. When a new Depreciation Report comes out, and the CIR is adjusted upwards, all future expenditures will increase in value dramatically. A sudden decrease in the reserve adequacy ratio makes the complex look financially weak.

Over-estimating the CIR will result in the complex appearing to have not enough money, with the possibility of decreasing the market value of the individual unit. This is because, as time passes, the inflated costs of the building components will be artificially increased, with the current requirement looking insufficient. Special levies larger than indicated in the Depreciation Report will be required.

Using the Annual Inflation Rate (AIR) as the CIR

The CIR is averaged over a longer term, so sudden economic changes are not utilized for long-term projections. The AIR can fluctuate year to year and take in the sudden economic changes the CIR tries to avoid.

Using the Canadian Price Index (CPI)

The construction cost inflation forecasts must be based on construction indices rather than the Consumer Price Index (CPI). The CPI measures the cost of a basket of consumer goods, like groceries, gas, rent and clothes.

The CPI is a short-term number representing a monthly, quarterly, or annual price change. The CIR represents medium-term construction price trends.

Changing the CIR Rate over Time

The CIR must always be stable for modelling purposes.

Changing the CIR percentage rate over the projection period is based on the provider's personal beliefs about the future, not relying on reliable historical data in the past.

Allowing Clients to Choose the CIR

The CIR is based on professional research, which council members usually do not have the time or expertise to determine. Client-based estimates usually lead to wishful thinking, resulting in a major underestimation of the CIR. In my opinion, it is also outside the legislation's intent.

Investment Interest Rate (IIR)

The second variable is the IIR. Investment interest income can be a significant and increasing source of revenue for the CRF. The cash and investments must be continuously and prudently invested to maximize income.

The CRF has a mixed allocation of investments and cash. The Strata Property Act requires funds to be invested in a limited group of "safe" investments, including term deposits, guaranteed investment certificates (GICs), or government bonds.

The investment interest rate (IIR) is based on the cash–investment allocation mix or the actual rate of return that a Strata Corporation gets in its CRF.

Given that cash receives an interest rate of approximately 0.1% and a GIC at 3.0%, the interest income that a CRF will receive is always between these two numbers. The less cash, the higher the IIR will be. As such, the best method to determine the IIR is to review the historical return rate of the last two to three years. Historically, in smaller complexes, the IIR is around 1.0%.

All funding plans need a stable IIR to be fiscally responsible and included in financial models. The IIR can change with new data in the subsequent report.

Common Investment Interest Rate Errors and Consequences

Over or under-estimating the IIR

To underestimate the IIR is difficult and usually never happens.

Under-estimating the IIR will result in a low-interest revenue report. The Strata will require more revenue from contributions, higher special levies, and possibly a loan to make up the shortfall. This indication that the complex will need more income may scare off some potential buyers.

Over-estimating the IIR frequently happens as it gives the appearance that the Corporation is in better financial shape than it actually is. This results in more interest income being projected in the report than reasonable. More special levies will be required when the interest income fails to materialize. This may create a real hardship for unprepared owners.

Other common errors are as follows:

Projecting Returns Based on GIC Rates

We have seen reports where the IIR is projected to increase because the provider has estimated a smaller percentage of cash in the CRF and a greater percentage of higher-income investments, such as GICs. This exercise increases the IIR rate and is theoretical without support.

The CRF account's historical interest returns should determine the projected investment interest rate. The provider can review and change the IIR once the report is updated.

Changing the IIR Rate over Time

The IIR must always be stable for modelling purposes and based on historical data. Changing the IIR rate over time is a speculative forecasting exercise.

Calculating Interest Monthly

Depreciation Reports are a budget-planning tool. Some reports have become very complicated, calculating interest based on the opening balance plus 50% of the annual contributions, less 50% of the expenditures for that year.

This method will always over-estimate the interest revenue as it relies on three unsupportable assumptions:

1. Everyone pays their strata fees and special levies on time. This payment scenario usually never occurs, so all revenue assumptions to earn interest are incorrect.

2. All special levies are paid in 12 equal payments.

3. All invoices are paid in equal installments over the year. This assumption is not based on reality. Most significant work is usually done in the summer for weather concerns. This seasonal nature of costs will deplete the CRF account, mainly during four months. Therefore, the report cannot support the bank account level projections.

Allowing Clients to Choose the IIR

In my opinion, allowing clients to choose their own IIR is outside the legislation's intent as it creates a report not based on a professional opinion. Our experience is that when clients determine the IIR, it usually leads to overestimation, as discussed above.

The 2 and 2 Problem

One of the most telling indicators that the provider does not understand the financial situation of the development is when they use the "2 and 2" methodology. Here, "2 and 2" means that the construction inflation rate (CIR) and the investment interest rate (IIR) are the same (i.e., 2% / 2%).

Most people understand that inflation will always be greater than interest income; therefore, this approach is never recommended.

Under-estimating inflation is always magnified in the long term, meaning the provider will minimize future costs. Inversely, the provider will overestimate the future revenue from interest. The net effect is that as time goes along, the report will become more unreliable, and the projected special levies will be greater than projected in the report. Providers and councils cannot mitigate this flaw if the percentages are higher at 2.5% / 2.5% or 3.5% / 3.5%. The net result is that some owners could be in financial hardship.

The provider must collect the financial documents to establish the correct percentages. While the Strata Property Regulations do not specify that the provider must choose the CIR and IIR, we see this problem when the provider lets the client set the CIR and the IIR. Usually, the client does not understand the implications, so they choose the same percentage.

Contribution Rate (CR)

The third variable is the CR. Contributions are the monthly or annual fees collected by the Strata Corporation as part of the yearly budget for the CRF account and are the primary source of revenue for the reserve fund. For the CRF to meet the recommended funding plan requirements, annual increases in the actual dollar amount are required in the projected 30-year timeframe.

The Contribution Rate (CR) is the annual rate of change of contributions, stated as a percentage, used in a Depreciation Report.

The second funding principle is that any development should have a stable contribution rate for financial modelling purposes and be equitable between the owners. Contribution rates that constantly increase or decrease over time violate the funding principles. They do not distribute costs evenly and are not fiscally responsible. This action usually occurs in the front or rear loading of the CRF, as described below.

A fiscally irresponsible cash flow will not be fair and equitable to owners. It will cause financial hardship as CRF contributions become harder to achieve later.

Councils and providers should set contributions for upcoming years before consideration of expected special levies, legal or insurance settlements, monies owed, or proposed operating budget surpluses planned to be transferred to the CRF. Transfers are all temporary and speculative. In addition, BC has legislation concerning excessive operating account surplus balances at the year's end and returning them to owners.

Contributions should be supplemented by special levies when additional funds are needed. Special levies are temporary and do not upset the steady contribution rate principle in the funding principles.

Owners must understand that in all funding plans, the year and the amount of the expected CRF expenses never change. The only items that change in a different funding plan are how they are paid for. Thus, their contribution rate may differ if other funding plans are presented.

Common Contribution Rate Errors and Consequences

Changing Rates of Contributions (Backloading the Report)

As discussed, there needs to be a stable contribution rate. If the contribution rate is 3%, it should remain at that percentage for the entire projection period.

I have read reports that backload the contributions when the contribution rate increases from a low rate in the first few years to a higher rate in the last few years.

An example is when the contribution rate is 3% in the first decade, increasing to 5% in the second decade and 8% in the third decade.

The concern is that this rate of growth will never occur. The increases in the last years of the 30-year forecast will be too high and never happen. The development will become uneconomic with increasing and higher special levies as time passes.

Changing Rates of Contributions (Front loading the report)

This occurs when the contribution rate decreases over time, say from 6% in the first decade to 3% in the second decade and 0% in the third decade. The issue here is the owners who do the math will not allow the increases to go through as they feel they are funding the future owners.

Developments getting their first report, or a report after an inflationary period, typically have a low CRF balance, meaning a short-term catch-up period is required. Later, the contribution rate is usually stabilized.

Optimum Contribution Rate (OCR)

The Optimum Contribution Rate (OCR) represents the annual contribution rate used in a Depreciation Report that will cover the loss in purchasing power due to inflation.

Below is the model for calculating the OCR, which requires the CIR and the IIR.

Optimum Contribution Rate (OCR)			
	Step 1	Step 2	Step 3
Investment Interest Rate (IIR)	1.0%		
Construction Inflation Rate (CIR)	3.0%		
Deduct the IIR from the CIR to Determine the Loss in Purchasing Power Due to Construction Inflation		3.0%-1.0% = 2.0%	
Add the CIR to the Loss in Purchasing Power to calculate the Optimum Contribution Rate (OCR)			3.0% + 2.0% = 5.0%

This model applies in all inflationary and deflationary cycles.

Renewal Assumptions

Within a Depreciation Report, the provider makes three assumptions.

Assumption 1: *Depreciation Reports assume components in all areas of the complex will be replaced at the same time, except if they are in a different phase.*

Depreciation Report providers understand that different areas of the building or property may be subject to accelerated wear and tear due to different weather exposure or usage. They also know owners can leverage economies of scale and thereby reduce the overall cost when completing a large project simultaneously. In other words, by completing a more extensive project at the same time, owners will save money on a per measurement unit (price per square foot, per door, per strata lot, etc).

Assumption 2: *Depreciation Reports assume related components will be replaced at the same time, even if some of the components could last longer due to being a different material.*

Providers will not replace every component separately if they are related. It is usually more economical and realistic to replace related components simultaneously. Therefore, the focus is creating an economic life that ends at the same time as the related items, as opposed to an actual lifespan.

An example is roofing, where the roofing material, hatches, skylights, vertical drainage, and flashing are usually done together on a low-slope roof. Failure to do something may have dramatic consequences. Not replacing flashing at the same time as the roofing material will usually invalidate a roofing warranty. Not replacing vertical drains when the roof is completed may result in uneven drainage, causing water to pool and possibly enter the roof frame.

Assumption 3: *Component description and costs are based on the understanding that the complex will replace all components with the same component type.*

Some items, like flooring replacement, only require a vote at the AGM. The assumption is "like for like", meaning if there was ceramic tile before, the flooring will be replaced with ceramic tile.

Anything visible to the general public, such as the exterior envelope siding materials, the roof and landscaping, usually needs a permit from the municipality or regional district. However, the "like for like" assumption is also appropriate here.

The one exception occurs when a building or similar code change disallows grandfathering. A great example is aluminum single-glazed windows. They were very common in older buildings but cannot be replaced as they have been banned for lack of heat efficiency. Therefore, all providers assume vinyl double-glazed windows are the replacements.

The other exception is when the council has done advanced work, like partial restoration of the siding of the building. This work is evidenced by a quote in place with a permit from the municipality or regional district.

In conclusion, understanding the critical importance of the CIR, the IIR, the CR and the renewal assumptions will help the owners identify and avoid incorrect financial modelling that can result in unreliable reports and economic hardship.

Chapter 20 – The Benchmark Analysis

The financial analysis aims to create a funding plan, but before that, the current and future replacement costs modelling is required. This costing is completed within the Benchmark Analysis, which connects the physical and financial analyses. For this reason, every professional standard for Depreciation Reports requires a Benchmark Analysis.

Once the components inventory is summarized, a chart of related costs is totalled. This chart begins with each component's current cost estimate being inflated with the CIR to their replacement dates. In other words, all components' life cycles and costs are calculated to understand the amount the Strata Corporation should save for current and future requirements.

As all costs are projected over 30 years, all the values are extremely sensitive to construction costs, inflation, and interest rate changes.

There are two underlying conditions in all Benchmark Analysis calculations.

The first condition is that the cost estimates have been prepared without regard to unit owners' current financial position or CRF contributions. As such, the Benchmark Analysis represents the optimum reserve fund operation, which assumes that the Strata Corporation is fully funded.

The second condition is the assumption that the complex will perpetually be renewed or go on forever. This condition is not valid in real life but is a critical assumption for modelling.

Under these two conditions, readers should recognize that the Benchmark Analysis is building-specific based on the condition at the time of inspection. These conditions mean two identical buildings with similar component costs, but different maintenance histories will have different calculations in the Benchmark Analysis. This is why a dollar value per square foot or per door is a poor indicator for comparative purposes.

Below is a list summarizing the definitions of all the costs calculated, their relationship to each other and some problems that we have seen in some reports.

Unit Price: The current replacement cost of an "age-defined" type component per unit of measurement. Examples are per square foot, linear foot, per unit, or a group of similar items usually called a package.

Allowances also have values, but as mentioned earlier, they are not the total replacement price, only a portion of the replacement value, as they are expected to last the life of the complex.

Current Replacement Cost: The cost of replacing, repairing, or restoring a reserve component to its original functional condition in the year of the inspection. The current replacement cost of a component is the Unit Quantity multiplied by the Unit Price.

Future Replacement Cost: The cost of replacing, repairing, or restoring the component to its original functional condition during the estimated replacement year. This represents the CIR inflated current replacement cost at the end of the expected lifespan. This value includes allowances.

Current Reserve Fund Requirement: The total CRF balance, based on the effective age of the component, that the owners should have contributed by the end of the first year of the report. In other words, how much money should be in the CRF account to replace this item if the CRF were fully funded?

The total Current Reserve Fund Requirement is critical as it is used to benchmark the reserve fund to determine Reserve Adequacy.

Future Reserve Fund Accumulation: The total amount that would need to be saved together with future interest income compounded over the remaining lifespan of the components for the balance of the funds required for the component to be paid for when it is estimated to be replaced. In other words, if the Strata Corporation saved the total Current Reserve Fund Requirement, how much more money would the owners need to replace the item?

Future Reserve Fund Requirement: This represents the owners' payments to the CRF fund plus any interest earned for future costs. These are the Future Replacement Costs, less the Future Reserve Fund Accumulations.

Annual Reserve Fund Contributions: Annual CRF contributions if the owners fully funded the development. This calculation is only for financial modelling and benchmarking to determine Reserve Adequacy and not as part of a recommended funding plan.

In some cases, the provider will break down the allocation of a specific component to the overall Annual Reserve Fund Contribution, as indicated on the chart on the following page. This is optional, but it does allow the reader to get an understanding of the expenses required.

Providers create confusion when they do not include unit costs or quantities and only list the current replacement cost. There is no method to calculate the measurements/unit quantities or cost going backwards. There is no transparency or ability to verify.

The Benchmark Analysis is split into 2 parts. The first part is the component inventory with the component lifespan and measurement data in Chapter 13. The second portion is the unit cost with the related six values required in a Depreciation Report. Below are the six sample values discussed above, followed by a complete Benchmark Analysis on the following page.

RESERVE COMPONENTS	YEAR OF ACQUISITION	EXPECTED LIFESPAN	EFFECTIVE AGE	REMAINING LIFESPAN	UNIT QUANTITY	UNIT MEASURE
Structural and Architectural						
1 Concrete Slab Foundation	1988	70	33	37	1	allowance
2 Vinyl Siding	1988	50	33	17	14228	square feet
3 Structural Wood Posts - Basic	1988	50	33	17	13	posts
4 Attached Service Room	1988	70	33	37	1	allowance
5 Window Assemblies	1988	35	34	1	78	windows
6 Window Assemblies (Large)	1988	35	34	1	10	windows
7 Metal Townhome Entrance Doors	2012	40	9	31	20	doors
8 Sliding Doors	2019	35	2	33	14	doors
9 Exterior Painting and Stain	2019	10	2	8	2500	square feet
10 Caulking and Waterproofing	2009	12	11	1	2600	linear feet
11 Exterior Powerwashing	2020	10	1	9	14500	square feet
12 Single Garage Door	1988	25	20	5	10	doors
Roofing						
13 Chimney Caps	2017	25	4	21	16	caps and/or chases
14 Asphalt Shingle	2017	25	4	21	14847	square feet
15 Skylights (20 X 46 inches)	2017	25	4	21	9	skylights
16 Wood Fascia	2001	25	20	5	1982	linear feet
17 Gutters and Downspouts	1996	25	20	5	1082	linear feet
18 Aluminum Soffits	1988	40	30	10	4378	square feet
Electrical Systems						
19 Cluster Subdivision Distribution System	2004	70	17	53	10	allowances (Per SL)
20 GFCI Outlets	1988	25	20	5	20	outlets
21 Exterior Lights and Outlets	2012	25	9	16	40	lights
Mechanical Systems						
22 Domestic Water Distribution Systems - Cluster	1988	70	35	35	2	allowances (Per SL)
23 Buried Sanitary and Storm Drainage System	1988	70	35	35	2	allowances
24 Natural Gas Fireplace Exhaust Fan	2000	25	17	8	4	units
Amenities						
25 Garage Interiors	1988	60	30	30	1	allowance
Site Improvements						
26 Exterior Paths and Patios	1988	50	33	17	2235	square feet
27 Concrete Driveways	1988	70	33	37	4900	square feet
28 Cedar Fencing Replacement	2005	24	16	8	544	linear feet
29 Cedar Fencing Restaining	2005	8	6	2	3264	square feet
30 Wood Fencing Replacement	2005	24	17	7	210	linear feet
31 Wood Fencing Repainting	2020	8	1	7	1260	square feet
32 Landscaping	2018	6	3	3	13418	square feet
33 Wood Trellis	2012	25	9	16	100	linear feet
Consultant Report						
34 Depreciation Report Renewal	2021	3	0	3	1	report
TOTAL RESERVES						

DEPRECIATION REPORTS IN BRITISH COLUMBIA

RESERVE COMPONENTS	YEAR OF ACQUISITION	EXPECTED LIFESPAN	EFFECTIVE AGE	REMAINING LIFESPAN	UNIT QUANTITY	UNIT MEASURE	UNIT COST	CURRENT REPLACEMENT COST	FUTURE REPLACEMENT COST	CURRENT RESERVE FUND REQUIREMENT	FUTURE RESERVE FUND ACCUMULATION	FUTURE RESERVE FUND REQUIREMENT	RESERVE FUND ANNUAL CONTRIBUTIONS
Structural and Architectural													
1 Concrete Slab Foundation	1988	70	33	37	1	allowance	$20,000.00	$20,000	$71,421	$9,429	$13,625	$57,796	$1,299
2 Vinyl Siding	1988	50	33	17	14228	square feet	$9.78	$139,150	$249,729	$91,839	$108,765	$140,964	$7,648
3 Structural Wood Posts - Basic	1988	50	33	17	13	posts	$720.00	$9,360	$16,798	$6,178	$7,316	$9,482	$514
4 Attached Service Room	1988	70	33	37	1	allowance	$2,000.00	$2,000	$7,142	$943	$1,363	$5,780	$130
5 Window Assemblies	1988	35	34	1	78	windows	$1,200.00	$93,600	$96,876	$90,926	$91,835	$5,041	$5,041
6 Window Assemblies (Large)	1988	35	34	1	10	windows	$1,800.00	$18,000	$18,630	$17,486	$17,661	$969	$969
7 Metal Townhome Entrance Doors	2012	40	9	31	20	doors	$900.00	$18,000	$52,291	$4,050	$5,513	$46,777	$1,295
8 Sliding Doors	2019	35	2	33	14	doors	$1,625.00	$22,750	$70,797	$1,300	$1,805	$68,991	$1,775
9 Exterior Painting and Stain	2019	10	2	8	2500	square feet	$1.99	$4,975	$6,551	$995	$1,077	$5,474	$661
10 Caulking and Waterproofing	2009	12	11	1	2600	linear feet	$2.80	$7,280	$7,535	$6,673	$6,740	$795	$795
11 Exterior Powerwashing	2020	10	1	9	14500	square feet	$2.97	$43,065	$58,693	$4,307	$4,710	$53,983	$5,762
12 Single Garage Door	1988	25	20	5	10	doors	$1,264.00	$12,640	$15,012	$10,112	$10,628	$4,385	$860
Roofing													
13 Chimney Caps	2017	25	4	21	16	caps and/or chases	$300.00	$4,800	$9,885	$768	$946	$8,939	$385
14 Asphalt Shingle	2017	25	4	21	14847	square feet	$13.40	$198,950	$409,723	$31,832	$39,229	$370,494	$15,943
15 Skylights (20 X 46 inches)	2017	25	4	21	9	skylights	$770.00	$6,930	$14,272	$1,109	$1,366	$12,905	$555
16 Wood Fascia	2001	25	20	5	1982	linear feet	$10.41	$20,633	$24,505	$16,506	$17,348	$7,157	$1,403
17 Gutters and Downspouts	1996	25	20	5	1082	linear feet	$11.95	$12,930	$15,357	$10,344	$10,872	$4,485	$879
18 Aluminum Soffits	1988	40	30	10	4378	square feet	$7.27	$31,828	$44,897	$23,871	$26,368	$18,528	$1,771
Electrical Systems													
19 Cluster Subdivision Distribution System	2004	70	17	53	10	allowances (Per SL)	$500.00	$5,000	$30,961	$1,214	$2,058	$28,903	$416
20 GFCI Outlets	1988	25	20	5	20	outlets	$135.00	$2,700	$3,207	$2,160	$2,270	$937	$184
21 Exterior Lights and Outlets	2012	25	9	16	40	lights	$150.00	$6,000	$10,404	$2,160	$2,533	$7,871	$456
Mechanical Systems													
22 Domestic Water Distribution Systems - Cluster	1988	70	35	35	2	allowances (Per SL)	$6,000.00	$12,000	$40,003	$6,000	$8,500	$31,503	$756
23 Buried Sanitary and Storm Drainage System	1988	70	35	35	2	allowances	$10,000.00	$20,000	$66,672	$10,000	$14,166	$52,506	$1,260
24 Natural Gas Fireplace Exhaust Fan	2000	25	17	8	4	units	$300.00	$1,200	$1,580	$816	$884	$697	$84
Amenities													
25 Garage Interiors	1988	60	30	30	1	allowance	$3,000.00	$3,000	$8,420	$1,500	$2,022	$6,399	$184
Site Improvements													
26 Exterior Paths and Patios	1988	50	33	17	2235	square feet	$9.01	$20,137	$36,140	$13,291	$15,740	$20,400	$1,107
27 Concrete Driveways	1988	70	33	37	4900	square feet	$24.00	$117,600	$419,953	$55,440	$80,115	$339,838	$7,635
28 Cedar Fencing Replacement	2005	24	16	8	544	linear feet	$80.56	$43,825	$57,709	$29,216	$31,637	$26,071	$3,147
29 Cedar Fencing Restaining	2005	8	6	2	3264	square feet	$1.77	$5,777	$6,189	$4,333	$4,420	$1,769	$880
30 Wood Fencing Replacement	2005	24	17	7	210	linear feet	$30.00	$6,300	$8,015	$4,463	$4,784	$3,231	$448
31 Wood Fencing Repainting	2020	8	1	7	1260	square feet	$1.85	$2,331	$2,966	$291	$312	$2,653	$368
32 Landscaping	2018	6	3	3	13418	square feet	$0.40	$5,367	$5,951	$2,684	$2,765	$3,186	$1,051
33 Wood Trellis	2012	25	9	16	100	linear feet	$45.00	$4,500	$7,803	$1,620	$1,900	$5,903	$342
Consultant Report													
34 Depreciation Report Renewal	2021	3	0	3	1	report	$1,587.42	$1,587	$1,760	$529	$545	$1,215	$401
TOTAL RESERVES								$924,215	$1,897,845	$464,383	$541,819	$1,356,025	$66,404

|117|

From this point, the provider can determine its recommended funding plan to meet the funding goal of the Strata Corporation. Funding plans are based on the funding models discussed in the following chapter. All funding models rely on the information in the Benchmark Analysis.

Below is a checklist so the reader can check their provider's report for the issues mentioned above.

	Benchmark Analysis Checklist	
√	**Column**	**Note or Comments in Report if not shown in the Benchmark Analysis**
☐	Unit Cost	
☐	Current Replacement Cost	
☐	Future Replacement Cost	
☐	Current Reserve Fund Requirement	
☐	Future Reserve Fund Accumulation	
☐	Future Reserve Fund Requirement	
☐	Annual Reserve Fund Contributions	

NOTES:

Chapter 21 – Measuring the Financial Health of My Complex

The following three chapters cover creating a funding plan. This chapter is designed to help Strata Corporations understand how to measure the financial health of their complex.

What Is Reserve Adequacy?

A reserve fund may be *adequate for a certain year* when the opening CRF balance, plus all the revenue or cash inflows (regular contributions, special levies, loan income, and interest income), provides sufficient cash for all possible cash outflows (reserve fund expenditures) required for repairing or replacing common elements or assets of the Strata Corporation. But this is not reserve adequacy.

Reserve Adequacy (or "Percent Funded") is the internationally accepted method for measuring the strength of the CRF. Reserve adequacy is a percentage ratio, expressed at the end of a fiscal year, of the actual (or projected) reserve balance as compared to the fully funded balance.

Another way to think about it is the amount the Strata Corporation is projected to have in cash at the end of the year, over what it would have if it were fully funded. The ratio indicates the ability of the Strata Corporation to adequately cover its expenditures at any given time.

How is Reserve Adequacy Calculated?

The key to the ratio is the Reserve Fund Requirement (RFR). The RFR represents the Current Reserve Fund Requirements as calculated in the Benchmark Analysis for year one, plus the net change annually to cover expenses. The annual change is based on the Annual Reserve Fund Contributions outlined in the Benchmark Analysis.

In other words, the RFR is the money that would be required to be in the bank at the end of a year to cover all future obligations if the Strata fully funded the reserve fund.

The RFR grows as the Strata Corporation's financial needs increase and as the components and other assets age. It shrinks when projects are accomplished and expenditures decrease. This figure is a moving but predictable target, changing annually. Therefore, knowing the RFR for each year is critical to long-term planning.

The RFR is difficult to calculate as it is essentially the sum of the present value of each component in the report when replaced. Readers do not need to be able to calculate the RFR, only to make sure that it is calculated in the Depreciation Report.

The reserve adequacy ratio is calculated in a two-step process:

First, calculate the Strata Corporation's RFR or what should be required in the bank today to cover all future obligations if the Strata Corporation fully funded the CRF.

Second, compare the current year-end CRF balance to the current year's RFR and express it as a percentage.

This is illustrated below:

Assume the Year End Balance in CRF is $38,000 and the projected RFR for the year is $350,000.

The Reserve Adequacy Ratio would be $38,000 / $350,000 or 10.857%.

This methodology considers the owners' annual income, whether by maintenance contributions, special levies, or loans, and the need to be accounted for in tandem with each year's ongoing reserve fund requirements. This knowledge allows the Strata Corporation to understand its financial requirements and to plan for these costs.

How Much Reserves Are Enough?

All providers are asked, *"How much money do we need in our CRF?"*

The answer is as much as is required to minimize your special levies in the future while meeting the ability of most owners to pay the annual maintenance fees. How we achieve this is discussed in the next chapter.

The reserve adequacy ratio is the best indicator of whether the CRF balance and contributions are sufficient. Below are the ranges we look for and their impact on owners.

Reserve Adequacy Greater Than 70%

This represents a strong Strata Corporation, typically funded through contributions only. Such developments are rare in British Columbia.

Reserve Adequacy Between 25% and 70%

This represents a Strata Corporation that focuses on increasing the monthly strata fees to the top of the range compared to similar developments. The goal is to minimize the amount and number of special assessments.

Developments that have just had a large project, like the envelope remediation on a leaky building or where major components were replaced or renewed, sometimes fall into this range. This is because the component may not need replacement during the remaining life of the complex and thus does not need to be saved for in the future.

Reserve Adequacy Between 10% and 25%

Our research indicates that most developments in British Columbia have a reserve adequacy between 10% and 25% of being fully funded. Many Strata Corporations have been using the reserve fund as an emergency fund and, due to substantial increases in items like insurance, have not maintained it. This is a poor financial strategy.

As discussed in the financial models in the next chapter, the lower the reserve adequacy ratio, the more frequent and higher the number of special levies the Strata Corporation will need. The focus should be on prioritizing increases in contributions to minimize reliance on more expensive funding methods.

Reserve Adequacy Less than 10%

Strata Corporations that are consistently below 10% do not have a realistic attitude toward the costs of renewal or replacement. Over time, some owners may sell at a discount or be forced into foreclosure as they cannot meet the financial demands.

After large expenditures, it is expected that the annual reserve adequacy rate is likely to dip below 10% before increasing again as contributions exceed expenditures in the following years.

There is currently no regulation that requires Strata Corporations to run tests to ensure that their reserve fund is adequate for its established purpose. A reserve fund deficiency or shortfall does not automatically mean that the reserve fund is inadequate. In concert with the report projections, it is up to the decision makers' judgment to determine whether the reserve fund funding model is sufficient to meet their responsibility to the Strata Corporation.

How Should I Compare One Property to Another?

For most people, the obligations in the next five to ten years are the most important to understand, as this will impact your cash flow and borrowing capacity the most. Understanding and planning for monthly reserve fund contribution increases and periodic special levies will provide realistic guidance. But the plan will become less reliable as it ages past ten years. For this reason, the legislation insists upon updates every 5 years.

Sometimes, one-time items like building envelope replacement or parking garage membrane replacement negatively affect the CRF balance and reserve adequacy. Readers need to understand that these items result from a proactive decision to stop further deterioration and should be embraced.

Comparing one property to another is a personal choice. Given this, look for the reserve adequacy ratio in the report and then focus on the strongest properties financially. If there is no reserve adequacy ratio in the report, ask the provider to calculate it or ask another firm for assistance.

Reserve Adequacy and the Impact on Market Value

All owners and buyers need to understand how the CRF impacts Market Value.

When thinking of a Depreciation Report, the value of the CRF is part of the value of the strata lot. Therefore, a potential buyer must know how to rate the CRF against other complexes. When measuring the CRF, readers must remember that the reserve adequacy ratio is building-specific, meaning buyers can compare multiple buildings.

The Local Market Indicator of Reserve Fund Averages (LMRFA) determines if the market will impact your unit. The LMRFA is the average reserve adequacy ratio within a market area. As indicated above, most developments are believed to have reserve adequacy between 10% and 25% of being fully funded in British Columbia, making this the LMRFA range within BC. The following chart outlines the general relationship between reserve adequacy and market value in the Lower Mainland and most likely elsewhere in British Columbia:

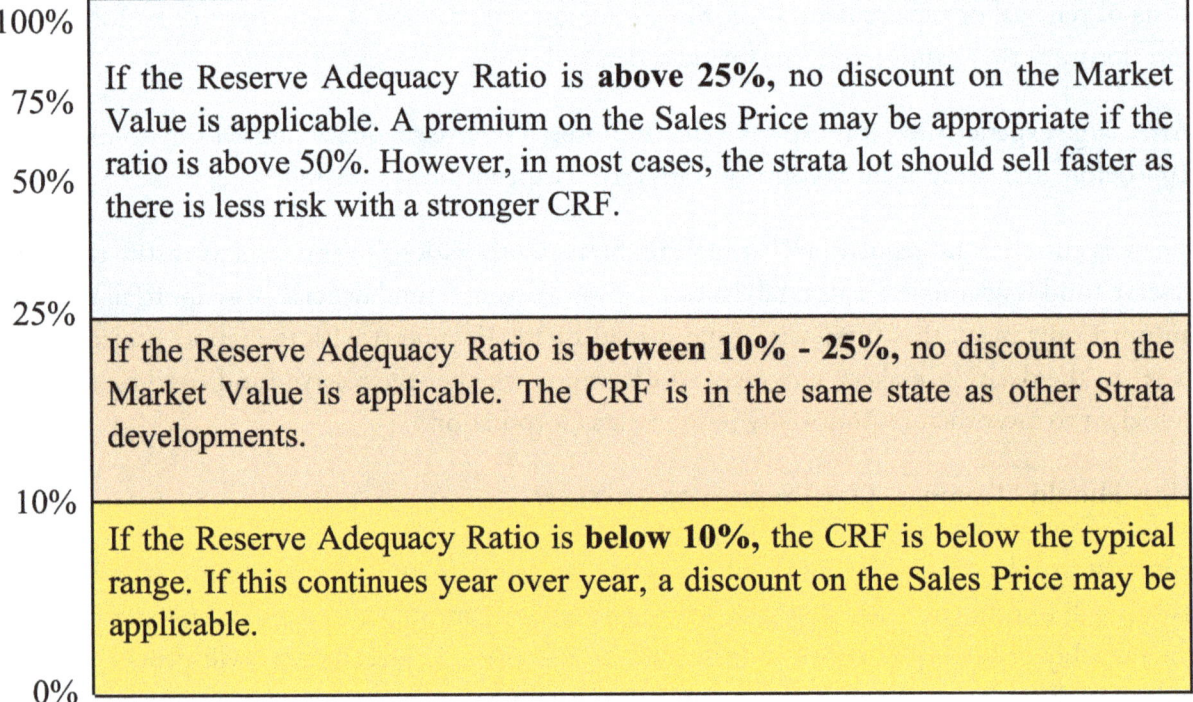

Just a note about Reserve Adequacy and newly constructed developments. These buildings sell for a premium price in the presales stage, usually with a reserve adequacy ratio below 10%. Presale buyers generally purchase for reasons other than simply occupying them. They hope the market will increase so they can assign (sell) the contract before possession or renting them out as investments. Presale buyers should be aware that they cannot compare reserve adequacy ratios to make informed decisions, as no Depreciation Report is required in the presale stage.

Is A High Reserve Adequacy Ratio Required in Older Buildings?

As funding models assume a perpetual life for the structure, assistance from the provider can help the council work towards a more realistic reserve strength target based on the age of the complex and the condition of its assets or components. Chapter 23 provides a more detailed explanation.

Chapter 22 – Generally Accepted Funding Plan Models

There are five generally accepted funding plan models currently in use by Strata Corporations throughout North America that allow similar terminology and methodology that promote transparency and comparability.

Funding Models

1. Fully Funded Model
2. Threshold Funded Model
3. Baseline Funding Model
4. Pay As You Go Funding Model
5. Statutory Model

Depending on your provider, one generally accepted model may be used. However, it is equally possible that a non-comparable model is in use. This inconsistency has caused three main problems.

Readers are confused, as some of the terminologies are not similar. Some language is based on legislation. Some terms are words used across the industry. Some terminology used in Canada is corporate-based, meaning the providers' firms choose what to call them. The result is that different providers have been using different names for similar models, as terminology across BC or Canada has not been standardized.

This lack of agreement has led to no standard definitions or agreed characteristics for the funding plan models. Firms have created models that incorporate some of the errors discussed in the book into their models.

As a result, some providers' funding models are not transparent and do not allow benchmarking, a requirement to calculate Reserve Adequacy, which was discussed in the prior chapter. These corporate models do not work into the generally accepted models utilized by professional reserve planning organizations outside Canada and standards-based providers in Canada.

So, what makes a funding plan model generally accepted?

A generally accepted funding model is one that is used by many firms and allows the creation of a benchmarking tool for measuring the financial health of a Strata Corporation. Reserve Adequacy is the most accepted benchmarking tool throughout North America for measuring the financial health of a development.

These are the five generally accepted models. The fully-funded model is a default model, as the data from the Benchmark Analysis (Schedule A, as shown in Chapter 20) will provide this funding plan model with no manipulation.

Fully Funded Model:

This model sets the reserve fund at 100%, being fully funded for the projection period.

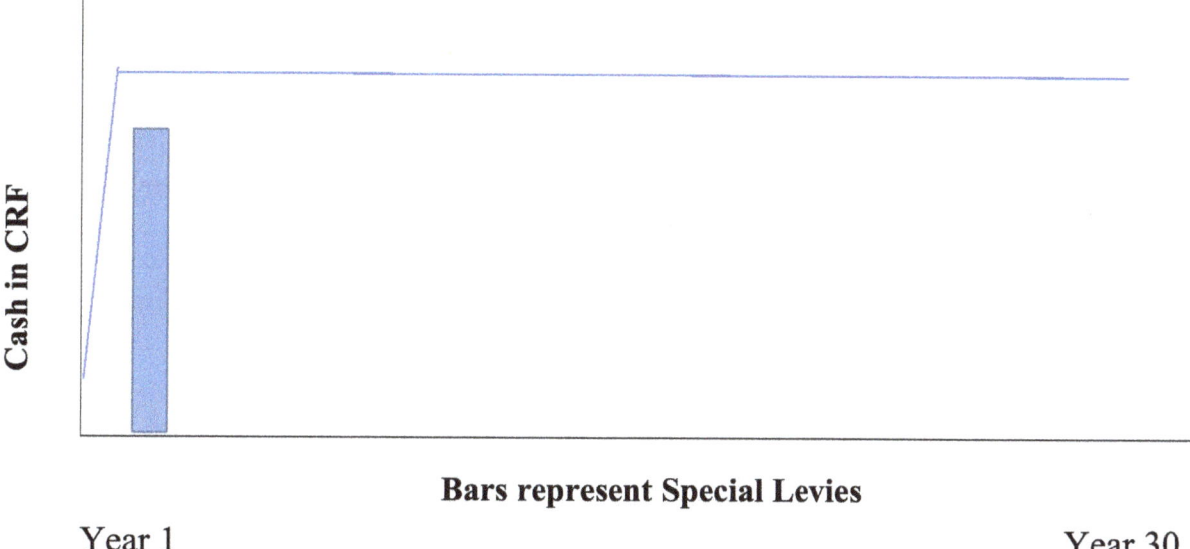

Bars represent Special Levies

Year 1   Year 30

Within the fully funded model, the Strata Corporation pays a one-time special levy to account for past deferred CRF contributions. Then, the Strata Corporation makes stable contributions to keep the CRF fully funded at or near 100% reserve adequacy. This model is also called the Benchmark model.

The catch is that the CRF fees are incredibly high, too expensive for most Strata Corporations to maintain. It would also make selling your strata lot difficult as your maintenance fees would be much higher than competitive developments.

The benchmark analysis creates the fully funded model by default. This information allows for calculating the RFR and Reserve Adequacy, with the ability to compare your development to others.

Common Fully Funded Model Errors and Consequences

Some providers name their model "fully funded" if it meets only one or two required characteristics instead of all three. The three characteristics are:

1. There is a large special levy in year one or two and no special levies afterward.
2. There is a significant increase in the annual CRF contributions, with stable contributions afterward.
3. Reserve Adequacy is at or near 100% annually after the special levy.

Some providers have stated that fully funded means that the Strata Corporation reserve adequacy must be 100% at the end of the projection period. However, this is not logical as it violates the funding principles because it needs to be more stable and evenly distributed.

This type of fully funded plan is also an illusion. When the report is updated every few years, the year the owners will fully fund the Strata Corporation will move to the end of the new projection period. In other words, the contributions will continually be backloaded and unrealistic.

Another provider changes the level of contributions (higher and lower) to meet the fiscal requirements of the year. Essentially, they are adding special levies when required but calling them contributions. Besides not being fully funded, this plan is designed to fail as the owners enthusiastically approve decreases but hesitate to approve the increases.

Still, another provider has defined fully funded as meaning when there are enough contributions to cover all the expenses in 30 years. This method appears on the cover to make sense. Assuming that the contributions bring in $1,000,000 over 30 years and the expenses are $999,999, meaning there will be a year-end CRF balance of $1.00 at the end of 30 years. The Strata Corporation will have covered its costs with all their contributions without special levies.

The problem is when a significant component, like the siding, needs to be replaced in year 31. The above model does not consider the future cash requirements needed to replace items. It is focused on expenses in the 30 years only. The other problem is that the percent funded is only calculated once, not annually. This method does not allow the owners to understand where they are financially during the projection period.

In all the above cases, as they are not correctly constructed fully funded models, they cannot be benchmarked by any accepted method.

Two of the funding models are based on proactive management. These are the Threshold Funded Model and the Baseline Funded Model. They are proactive as their use indicates a certain amount of long-term planning by the council members.

Threshold Funded Model:

This model focuses on setting a funding plan goal of being funded between 0% and 100% and then concentrating on increasing the strength as a percentage over time. The funding measurement tool is reserve adequacy.

All Strata Corporations are deficient financially, meaning the CRF account is underfunded. This situation results from paying less than what was required in the past. These contributions are deferred to later when special levies are periodically needed to make up for the shortfalls. Under this model, as the CRF reserve adequacy strengthens as a percentage, the special assessments should decline in frequency and amount.

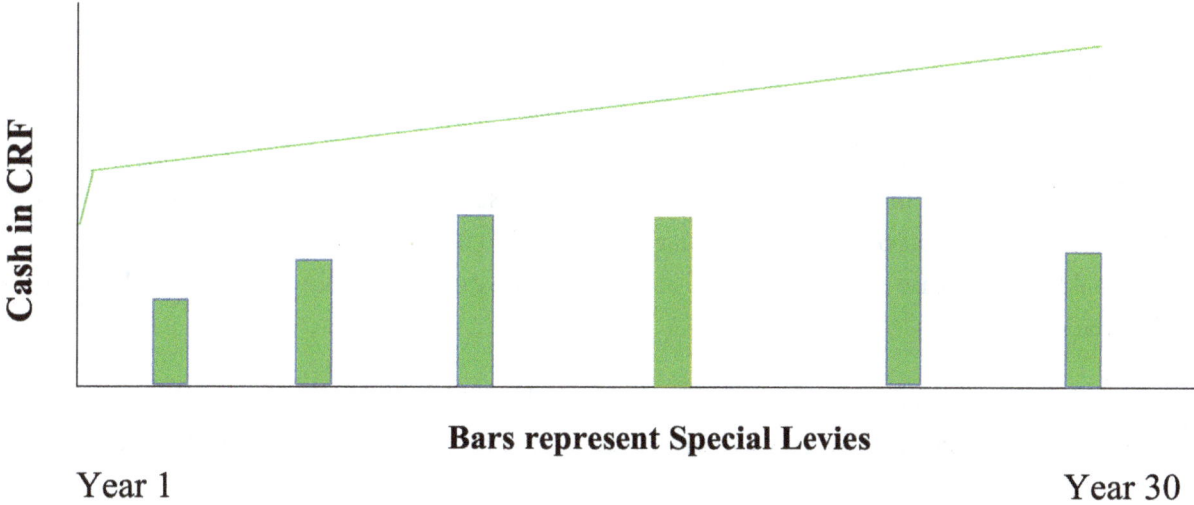

The Threshold Funded Model allows the owners to understand the risk of special levies and to choose financial options that enable them to remain competitive.

In BC, many providers provide multiple funding plan variations of this model, only changing the contribution rates in each plan.

This model is the preferred funding method of many providers.

Baseline Funded Model:

This model focuses on setting a reserve funding goal of keeping the projected annual reserve fund closing balances at or above a specified dollar amount arbitrarily chosen by the owners.

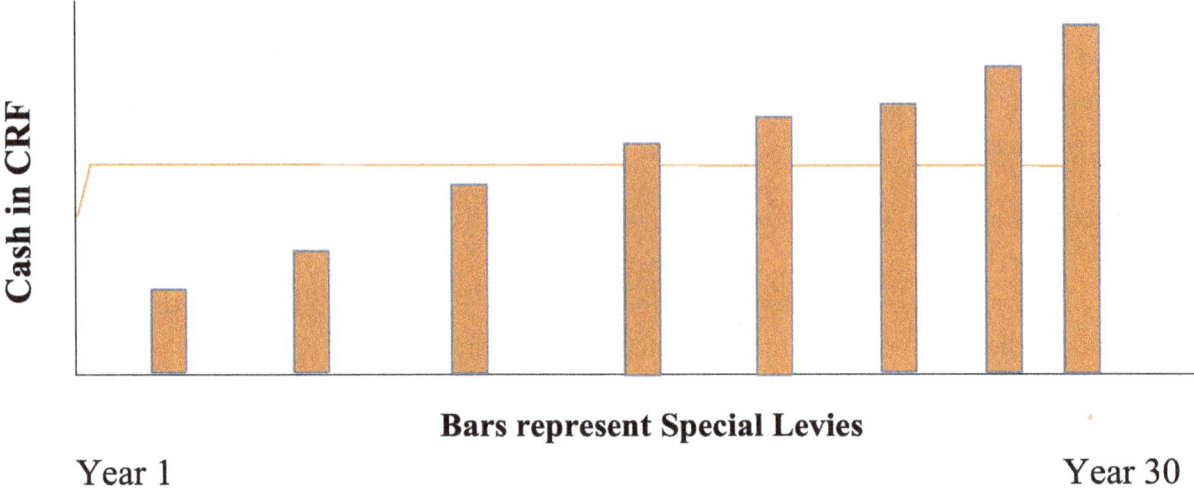

Bars represent Special Levies

Year 1   Year 30

The concern with this model is that the dollar figure may be too low. While $100,000 may be sufficient in year 1, as inflation eats away at the purchasing power of the CRF balance, in real dollars, the same amount of reserve funds may be worth $20,000 to $30,000 in year 30. As time goes on, special levies increase in frequency and amounts as the purchasing power of the CRF decreases with inflation.

In cases where the owners insist providers benchmark the balances, the reserve adequacy starts high and declines over time. The owners will only know if they are competitive within the local area by comparing monthly strata fees.

This approach is riskier for owners, as experience has shown that this method tends to fail to meet reserve fund requirements, with increasing special levies in volume and amount. As such, most providers do not recommend this model to clients.

The final two funding plan models are based on reactive management in that long-term planning is minimal. Funding choices like special levies and loans, or options including deferred maintenance, are suddenly thrust upon owners as emergencies increase to maintain the building.

"Pay as You Go" with Special Levies Model:

This is the current model in most Strata Corporations today.

In this case, the Strata Corporation will continue following its current funding plan goal. The result is that the complex typically does not have sufficient money to cover expected replacement costs. The only recourse is to schedule special levies to cover these costs on a reactive basis.

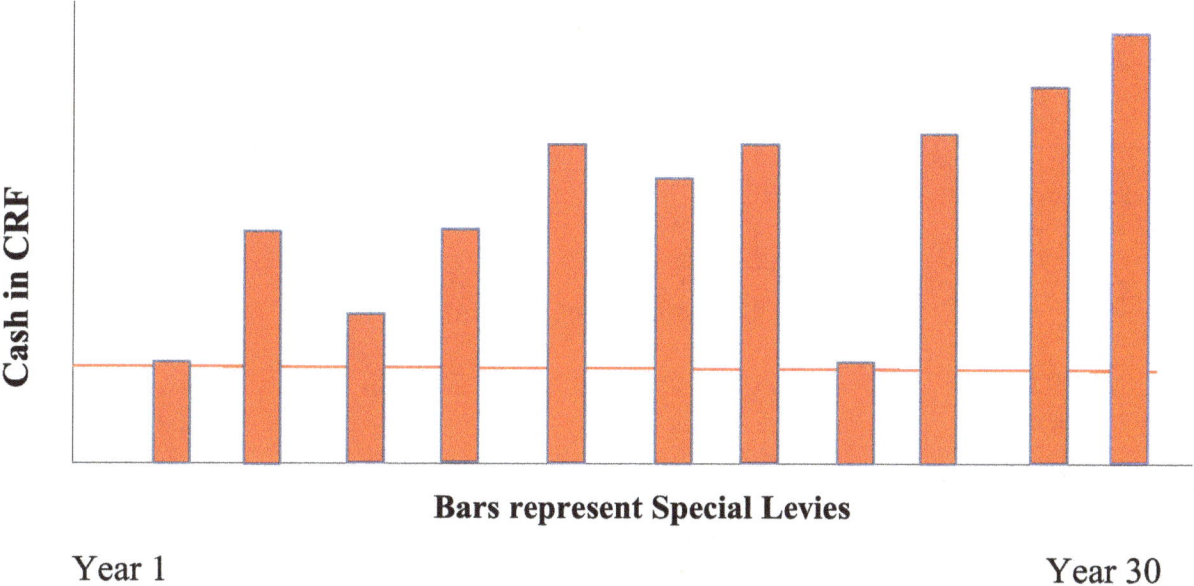

Bars represent Special Levies

Year 1   Year 30

These Strata Corporations usually do not know how to improve, or the owners do not have the financial capacity to increase the contributions to improve the reserve adequacy ratio. Therefore, special levies will continually be higher and more frequent as time passes.

This model is not based on funding the actual needs for the development and, therefore, is usually not recommended. Providers encountering this model typically like to move the Strata Corporation to a more proactive model in the future as the recommended funding plan model.

Statutory Funded Model:

All provinces have legislation regarding minimal funding levels that must be transferred to the CRF. As of November 1, 2023, BC has legislation that the annual CRF contribution must equal 10% of the annual Operating Budget. There is no upper limit to where the Strata Corporation can stop contributing, nor minimum balance required.

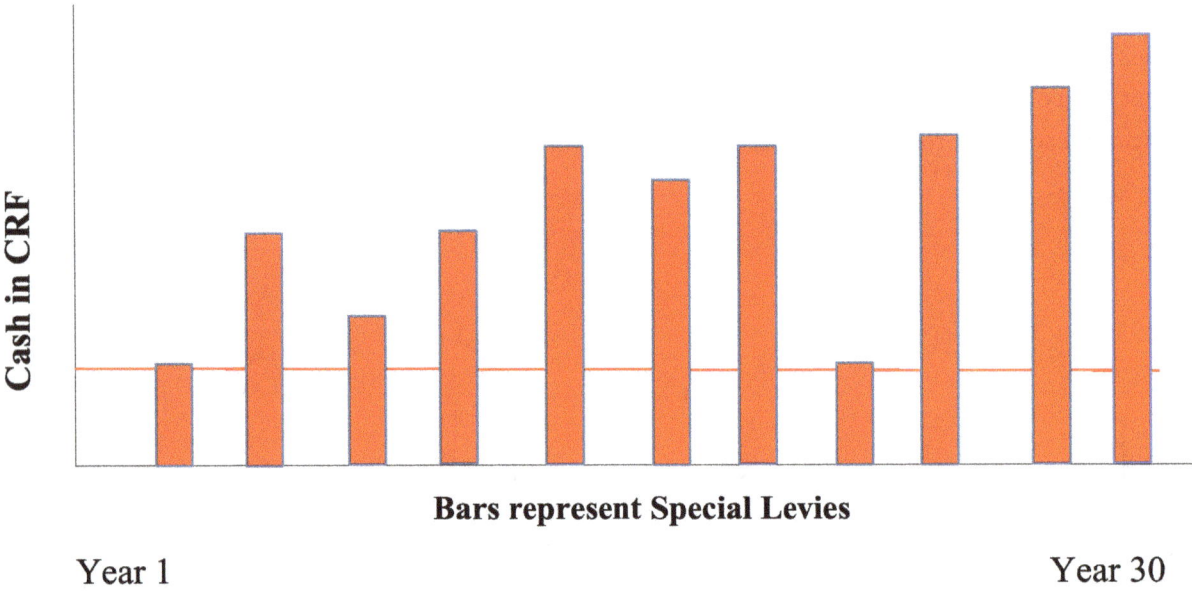

This model is the riskiest of the financial models and could jeopardize the economic viability of the development if special levies cannot be raised when needed.

The Statutory Funding and "Pay As You Go" models can lead to a "Catch-22" scenario. Due to constant special levies, the owners cannot increase the annual contributions. As the building gets older, the funding requirements get more significant and will add more strain on the owners. The result is a downward spiral that ends with decreasing market values, a lack of ability to get mortgages for potential buyers, and finally, an early termination of the Strata Corporation.

This scenario happened in Surfside, Florida, to the Champlain Towers South, as shown in Chapter 2. Essentially, the owners minimized the annual contributions for many years and could not afford the special levies when required. Without the money necessary, maintenance was not completed, and the building fell down.

Chapter 23 – Making a Recommended Funding Plan

All clients and readers have one crucial question - *how will the recommended funding plan be determined?*

As stated earlier, a standards-based approach is recommended in all reports as it allows Reserve Adequacy to measure the financial health of the complex.

First, all providers determine the opening CRF balance. All Depreciation Reports must indicate the starting balance in the reserve account. It will be the same in all funding plans provided in the report.

Next, the complex's operating budget is estimated for the next 30 years, based on the increases in the past few years. A statutory contribution level of 10% of the estimated operating budget sets the minimum contribution levels. The report should have a 30-year chart estimating the projected operating budgets and statutory funding levels.

Then, the development's monthly contributions are calculated based on the opening balance, increasing by the contribution rate (CR) choice but excluding any special levies. The annual contributions must equal or exceed the 10% amount calculated above in all funding plans.

When determining the recommended level of contributions, there are three numbers many planners review. They are the current contribution level, the monthly ASL contributions target, and reserve adequacy.

ASL (Average Strata Lot) represents the total cash inflows (contributions and special levies) recommended in a year divided by the number of lots without consideration for strata lot size or the unit of entitlement. A few firms have called this ACL (Average Contribution Level), which is misleading as it does not include special levies. Providers do not use the Unit of Entitlement for each strata lot, as the goal is to determine averages.

The first indicator is the past years' contributions and their relationship to ASL targets, as measured in dollars. Most experienced providers, standards-based or not, will focus on this model.

For example, in my firm, as of 2024, the target for monthly ASL contributions is $50 monthly for bare land developments. It may seem high, but the cost of roadway replacement is also exceptionally high. The amounts differ based on the needs of each type of property.

The second indicator is their current reserve adequacy ratio. This method is the focus of standards-based providers.

If the reserve adequacy ratio is below 10% in the first year, the first goal is to get the complex above 10% and keep it above this baseline. When it is above 10% at the beginning, the goal is to make it stronger. Unlike ASL calculations, this measurement tool is building-specific.

In a scenario where the current contributions (ASL) are meager, the CRF balance will usually be deficient, reflected in a low reserve adequacy ratio.

Increasing the contributions is an art, but some general guidelines exist.

First, a significant increase in monthly contributions is required in many cases. Typical increases are between 50% to 200% in developments with contribution levels that are too low. Anything above this is simply unrealistic.

Second, if a major project requires a large special levy in the first three years, an increase beyond the contribution rate is never applied in the same year as the levy. It looks great on paper but will never be accepted by the owners.

This method should allow the ASL contributions to reach most target levels within the first five years. Then, the focus becomes on increasing reserve adequacy.

Using special levies instead of regular contributions to raise the reserve adequacy ratio will also improve the CRF balance and reserve adequacy ratio. Still, it will not affect the ASL levels. It is an unrealistic situation because it requires a separate vote annually, which over time tends to fail due to special levy fatigue.

After getting to a realistic contribution level, the focus becomes improving reserve adequacy. As mentioned earlier, the goal of the Depreciation Report is to strengthen the fiscal health of the development through prudent financial planning. This task is done by increasing the reserve adequacy ratio over time, which results in lower and fewer special levies.

But it does not mean the path will be steady. As major expenditures occur, the reserve adequacy ratio will decline and then be raised when contributions exceed expenses. Recommended funding plans usually include special levies.

When thinking about special levies, I break them into major, minor, and typical.

I consider a major special levy major if it is over 5% of the sale price of the last sale in the development. If the previous sale in the complex were $500,000, anything over $25,000 per strata lot would be classified as such. These special levies are usually restricted to years when major programs, such as envelopes or underground membrane repairs, are required. Still, the CRF needs to be increased to cover the costs.

Using the example above, minor special levies are those under 1% of the last unit sold or under $5,000 per unit. This level is often used when the council wants to keep the reserve adequacy ratio level instead of letting it decline when an expenditure is required.

A typical special levy is between a minor and a major levy.

Experienced planners should have strategies regarding the application of special levies.

Several special levies may be appropriate within ten years when the reserve adequacy is low, as discussed earlier in the book. Professionals will try to spread out more significant special levies. If there are a few smaller levies, they are sometimes merged, so one moderate levy will occur rather than several consecutive small levies.

One of the most important guidelines is that special levies should never exceed the total expenditures in the same year. While it will increase the reserve adequacy ratio, it will never be approved. Given that it is unrealistic, professionals should never put this into a report.

Several small levies over a brief time are also unrealistic, leading to special levy fatigue and loss of credibility. After all, if there are five consecutive years of levies, why not just increase monthly contributions?

All professionals do their best to create a recommended funding plan based on their understanding of the current situation while following strategies to meet ASL targets that will increase reserve adequacy.

A Discussion about British Columbia and the Three Funding Plans:

Three funding plan scenarios are required in British Columbia. Every other province, territory or state in North America has only one recommended funding plan required. This is so the owners can concentrate on the provider's plan instead of getting confused.

Some firms provide as many as five funding plan scenarios, with varying contribution levels, providing different choices. These many choices can lead to disagreement among owners as they fight over the version they want. While allowable within the legislation, this concept is flawed when the contribution rate has no relationship to the optimal contribution rate or any historical increases. In these cases, I see reports when the contribution rate is too high to be accepted, like 10% to 15% annually. There is zero chance of acceptance.

BC has no legislation stating that providers should recommend one of the three funding plans. The result is some planners will not focus the report on one plan. Professional planners always have one recommended funding plan in the report so the Strata Corporation can concentrate on the provider's recommendations.

If there is a recommended plan, the other options may be alternate recommendations or only for educational purposes. The only requirement is that the contributions exceed the minimum statutory funding level. There is no legislation stating they must be realistic.

All Strata Councils should demand that their reports have a recommended funding plan and that the provider show the reserve adequacy in all scenarios. This requirement would give owners more realistic guidance and comparable funding scenarios.

Dealing With End-of-Life Funding

Termination is when the owners vote to end the life of the condominium or Strata Corporation. As discussed earlier, financial modelling assumes that the building will last forever, although everyone understands this is unrealistic.

Most people agree that wood frame buildings will last up to around 80 years, while concrete and brick buildings are usually expected to last 100 years. Between 25 and 35 years is the first cycle of roofing, windows, and some siding repairs. The next major cycle of repairs is 25 to 35 years later. A wood-framed building usually does not have a third cycle of roof repairs. In a concrete structure, the third roof is a significant indicator, as this is usually around 50% to 75% of the typical building life.

To account for this, in a wood-framed structure, many providers will reduce the contribution rate after the second cycle of repairs. Sometimes, the contribution rate is reduced to zero, meaning the monthly fees do not change in the plan year over year.

The reasoning is based on real-life motives. Owners do not want to save for a repair that will never occur. Once understood, owners typically will not approve increases in CRF fees if they feel they are in the end-of-life cycle of the building. The only thing stopping owners from going to no contributions is the statutory minimums as required under the legislation.

The other reason termination occurs is when the land use plan for the area supports a density much higher than what it is on the site presently, making the land value greater than the total market value of all the units. Providers are not allowed to account for this in their reports.

This book represents many people's experiences and over a decade's worth of reports. It provides all the information a Strata Council member or an Owner needs to choose their provider and get a standards-based report. Good luck.

APPENDIX A - TERMS AND DEFINITIONS

ACL (Average Contribution Level): See ASL.

ANNUAL INFLATION RATE (AIR): The annual increase in construction costs used in insurance appraisal reports. It is a short-term rate and reflects the sudden change in pricing (due to shortage or lack of demand) that may not be replicated over several years.

ANNUAL RESERVE FUND REQUIREMENT: Annual CRF contributions if the owners fully funded the development. This calculation is only for financial modelling and benchmarking to determine Reserve Adequacy.

ASL (Average Strata Lot): ASL (Average Strata Lot) represents the total cash inflows (contributions and special levies) recommended in a year divided by the number of lots without consideration for size or unit of entitlement.

ALLOWANCES: Some of the individual line items in the Depreciation Report physical analysis are for a type of component category that accounts for events that may or may not occur. Allowances, such as a concrete slab in a townhome complex, have an expected lifespan normally equal to or beyond that of the complex's physical life. It is prudent to have some savings in the reserve fund for these events so that if they do happen, funds are available.

Because there is a small probability that the component will need replacement during the development's life, a small portion of the full replacement amount is used. In addition, as it is not foreseeable that it will be used, allowances are never expensed in the cash flow documents.

ASSETS: These are components that are not attached to the building and can be picked up and moved. They are commonly called Furniture, Fixtures and Equipment (FF&E). If you have any, this list includes items in the lobby, laundry room, gym, pool, kitchen, common areas, and guest suites. See COMPONENTS.

BENCHMARK ANALYSIS: The Benchmark Analysis summarizes the component inventory, with the current and future replacement costs adjusted by the CIR and IIR. It also calculates the projected annual contribution if the owners have fully funded the Strata Corporation. This schedule is the key to assessing the financial state of the Strata Corporation and creating a recommended funding plan.

APPENDIX A - TERMS AND DEFINITIONS

BARE LAND STRATA REGULATIONS: The Bare Land Regulations are authorized by the *Strata Property Act* to regulate Strata Plan developments with a single-dimensional parcel. See STRATA PROPERTY ACT and STRATA PROPERTY REGULATIONS.

BYLAWS: These provide for the administration of the Strata Corporation and the control, management, maintenance, use and enjoyment of the strata lots, common property, and common assets of the Strata Corporation. Bylaws can impact a Depreciation Report. See STRATA PROPERTY ACT

CASH FLOW FUNDING METHOD: The method of developing a funding plan where contributions to the CRF are designed to offset the annual expenditures as pooled funds. With council approval, pooled CRF monies can be moved around. Different reserve funding plans are tested against the anticipated schedule of reserve expenditures until the desired funding goal is achieved. All Strata Corporations use this method in BC.

COMPONENT: The individual line items in the Depreciation Report developed or updated in the physical analysis. These items form the building blocks for a Depreciation Report. Components typically are:

1. A Strata Corporation responsibility.
2. With limited expected lifespan expectancies.
3. With predictable remaining lifespan expectancies, and
4. With a cost above a minimum threshold.

Components can also refer to items attached to the building, such as siding, roofing, doors, hallway carpeting, and landscaping.

COMPONENT FUNDING METHOD: The method of developing a funding plan where contributions to the CRF are separated based on each component. Theoretically, the money is dedicated to the asset or in a separate CRF account. Every component is fully funded each year. This method is the basis for calculating the Benchmark Analysis before using the Cash Flow Funding Method for operating the CRF.

COMPONENT INVENTORY: The task of selecting and quantifying reserve components. The inventory lists all the major components and assets that the Strata Corporation is responsible for maintaining, such as exterior walls, roofing, hallways, elevators, amenity rooms, and parking. The provider can accomplish this task through on-site visual observations, a review of Strata Corporation design and organizational documents, prior reports, and a discussion with the appropriate Strata Corporation representative(s).

CONDITION ANALYSIS: The portion of the component inventory where the current condition of the component being reported on is evaluated based on observed or reported characteristics.

APPENDIX A - TERMS AND DEFINITIONS

CONTINGENCY RESERVE FUND (CRF): The fund required under the *Strata Property Act* and Regulations for Strata Corporations' long-term major repair and replacement of common property assets. The other bank account required is the OPERATING ACCOUNT.

CONTRIBUTIONS: The monthly or annual fees collected by the Strata Corporation as part of the annual budget for the CRF account. They exclude interest income, special levies, proceeds from a strata loan (borrowings) or transfers at the year-end from an operating budget surplus.

CONTRIBUTION RATE (CR): The annual rate of change of contributions, stated as a percentage, used in a Depreciation Report.

CRF BALANCE: The amount of money in the CRF at a particular time. Financial planning requires the reserve fund (CRF) opening balance, while the reserve adequacy ratio calculations require the year-end balance.

CONSTRUCTION INFLATION RATE (CIR): The projected inflation rate of construction costs in the 30-year projection.

CURRENT REPLACEMENT COST: The cost of replacing, repairing, or restoring a reserve component to its original functional condition in the year of the inspection.

CURRENT RESERVE FUND REQUIREMENT: The total CRF balance, based on the effective age of the component, that the owners should have contributed by the end of the first year of the report. In other words, how much money should be in the CRF account to replace this item if the CRF were fully funded?

DEFICIT: An actual (or projected) reserve balance less than the fully funded balance. The opposite would be a surplus.

DEFICIENCY: This term means insufficient funds in the CRF to be deemed fully funded.

DEPRECIATION REPORT: A budget-planning tool that identifies the reserve fund's current status and a stable and equitable funding plan to offset the anticipated future major common area expenditures. The Depreciation Report consists of two parts: the physical analysis and the financial analysis.

DEPRECIATION REPORT PLANNER: An individual or firm that prepares Depreciation Reports.

DEPRECIATION REPORT PROVIDER: see DEPRECIATION REPORT PLANNER.

EFFECTIVE AGE: The difference between expected lifespan and remaining lifespan. It is not always equivalent to chronological age since some components age irregularly.

APPENDIX A - TERMS AND DEFINITIONS

EXPECTED LIFESPAN: Total useful life or depreciable life. The estimated time, in years, that a reserve component can be expected to serve its intended function if properly maintained and constructed in its present application or installation.

FINANCIAL ANALYSIS: This portion of the Depreciation Report evaluates the Strata Corporation's CRF opening balance, history of contributions, prior interest income and the projected expenses in the Benchmark Analysis to determine the recommended funding plan. The financial analysis is one of the two parts of a Depreciation Report.

FULLY FUNDED: 100% funded. When the actual (or projected) reserve balance is equal to the fully funded balance.

FUND STATUS: The reserve fund status compared to an established benchmark such as percent funding.

FUNDING GOALS: Independent of the methodology utilized, the following represent the basic categories of funding plan goals:

1. **Full Funding**: setting a reserve funding goal of attaining and maintaining reserves at or near 100% funded.
2. **Threshold Funding**: establishing a reserve funding goal of keeping the reserve balance above a specified percent funded amount. Depending on the threshold, this may be more or less conservative than fully funded.
3. **Baseline Funding**: establishing a reserve funding goal of keeping the reserve cash balance above zero at a specified dollar amount.
4. **Pay As You Go" with Special Levies**: following the current funding plan goal and paying the special levies as they are required, and
5. **Statutory Funding**: establishing a reserve funding goal of setting aside the specific minimum amount of reserves required by the Strata Property Act.

FUNDING PLAN: A Strata Corporation's plan to provide income to a reserve fund to offset anticipated expenditures from that fund. The funding choices include annual CRF contributions, interest earned, special levies, or loans.

FUNDING PRINCIPLES:

1. Sufficient funds when required.
2. Stable contribution rate over the years.
3. Evenly distributed contributions over the years, and
4. Fiscally responsible.

APPENDIX A - TERMS AND DEFINITIONS

FUTURE REPLACEMENT COST: The cost of replacing, repairing, or restoring the component to its original functional condition during the estimated replacement year. This represents the CIR inflated current replacement cost at the end of the expected lifespan.

FUTURE RESERVE FUND ACCUMULATION: The total amount that would need to be saved together with future interest income compounded over the remaining lifespan of the components for the balance of the funds required for the component to be paid for when it is estimated to be replaced. In other words, if the Strata Corporation saved the full Current Reserve Fund Requirement, how much more money would the owners need to replace the item?

FUTURE RESERVE FUND REQUIREMENT: This represents the owners' payments to the CRF fund plus any interest earned for future costs. These are the Future Replacement Costs, less the Future Reserve Fund Accumulations.

INCOME Includes annual contributions, interest income, special levies, proceeds from a strata loan (borrowings), or transfers from the operating budget surplus at the year-end.

INVESTMENT INTEREST RATE (IIR): The projected rate of return in the CRF bank account is based on the cash–investment vehicle allocation mix.

LIFE CYCLE ESTIMATES: Estimating the expected lifespan or useful life, the effective age, the remaining lifespan and the repair or replacement costs for the reserve components.

LOCAL MARKET INDICATOR OF RESERVE FUND AVERAGES (LMRFA): The average reserve adequacy ratio within a market area.

OPENINGS: Anything that penetrates the exterior roof or envelope of the building, including doors, windows, sliding doors, skylights, vents, plugs, and gas and water hook-up bibs.

OPERATING ACCOUNT: This is the bank account required under the British Columbia Strata Property Act and Regulations for Strata Corporations' annual budget. The other bank account required is the CONTINGENCY RESERVE FUND (CRF).

PERCENT FUNDED: See RESERVE ADEQUACY.

PHYSICAL ANALYSIS: This involves collecting documents and inspecting the building components and assets to determine the component inventory, physical condition analysis, and life estimates of the building components and assets, which the Strata Corporation must maintain. This analysis represents one of the two parts of the Depreciation Report.

PHYSICAL DESCRIPTION: The portion of the component inventory where the components being reported on are described.

APPENDIX A - TERMS AND DEFINITIONS

PLANNER: see DEPRECIATION REPORT PLANNER.

PROVIDER: see DEPRECIATION REPORT PLANNER.

QUALIFIED PERSON: People designated in the Strata Property Act as qualified to complete Depreciation Reports. These firms and people are called Planners or Providers. As of July 1, 2024, the Strata Property Regulations defines a "Qualified Person" as:

1. A professional engineer registered as a member in good standing with the Association of Professional Engineers and Geoscientists of the Province of British Columbia;
2. A person registered as an architect with the Architectural Institute of British Columbia;
3. A person designated Accredited Appraiser Canadian Institute (AACI) by the Appraisal Institute of Canada;
4. A Certified Reserve Planner (CRP) accredited by the Real Estate Institute of Canada;
5. A person designated as a Professional Quantity Surveyor by the Canadian Institute of Quantity Surveyors; and
6. A person registered as an applied science technologist under the Professional Governance Act;

REMAINING LIFESPAN (RLS): The estimated time, in years, that a reserve component can be expected to continue to serve its intended function. Also referred to as remaining life (RL).

RESERVE ADEQUACY: The ratio, at the end of a fiscal year, of the actual (or projected) reserve balance as compared to the fully funded balance, expressed as a percentage. The ratio indicates the ability of the Strata Corporation to cover its expenditures at any given time.

RESERVE BALANCE: See CRF BALANCE.

RESERVE FUND: See CONTINGENCY RESERVE FUND.

RESERVE FUND REQUIREMENT (RFR): This represents the Current Reserve Fund Requirements as calculated in the Benchmark Analysis for the first year, plus the net change on an annual basis to cover expenses, as represented by the Annual Reserve Fund Contributions, also outlined in the Benchmark Analysis. In other words, the RFR represents what would be required in the bank at the end of a year to cover all future obligations if the Strata had fully funded the reserve fund.

RULES: Rules govern the use, safety, and condition of common property and assets. Rules cannot govern the use of strata lots; only bylaws can do this. See STRATA PROPERTY ACT.

RESERVE PLANNING: The process of creating a Depreciation Report for Strata Corporations.

SPECIAL LEVY: A cash amount collected from the members of a Strata Corporation in addition to regular contributions. The *Strata Property Act* and Regulations govern special levies.

STRATA PROPERTY ACT: The legislation governing the operation of Strata Corporations. The *Strata Property Act*, regulations and the Strata Corporation's bylaws and rules provide the legal framework under which all Strata Corporations, including strata-titled duplexes, must operate in British Columbia. Part 6 regulates the finances.

STRATA PROPERTY REGULATIONS: The Strata Property Regulations, or Minister's orders, are authorized by the *Strata Property Act* to regulate Strata Plan developments with multiple dimensional parcels. The Cabinet passes regulations as "Orders in Council" or "OICs" and are signed by the Lieutenant-Governor. The government may pass regulations at any time of the year without going through the Legislature. See STRATA PROPERTY ACT and BARE LAND STRATA REGULATIONS.

UNIT OF ENTITLEMENT: The method by contributions and special levies are allocated to each strata lot owner under the *Strata Property Act* or the *Condominium Act*, whichever was in place when the development was registered.

DEFINITION REFERENCE

The definition of technical reviews in Chapter 5 can be found https://www.lawinsider.com/dictionary/technical-review

www.ingramcontent.com/pod-product-compliance
Lightning Source LLC
Chambersburg PA
CBHW081158020426
42333CB00020B/2547